DRAMA

for the
dramatically
challenged

To Aunt Pat,

Thank you for your
love and encouragement
through the years. I love you!

Laura L. Martinez

DRAMA

for the dramatically challenged

CHURCH PLAYS MADE EASY

laura l. martinez

Judson Press
Valley Forge

Drama for the Dramatically Challenged: Church Plays Made Easy

Library of Congress Cataloging-in-Publication Data

Martinez, Laura L.
    Drama for the dramatically challenged : church plays made easy / Laura L. Martinez.
        p. cm.
    Includes index.
    ISBN 0-8170-1356-3 (pbk. : alk. paper)
    1. Drama in public worship. 2. Drama in Christian education. 3. Christian drama, American. I. Title.
    BV289.M37   2000
    246'.72–dc21   00-026741

Printed in the U.S.A.

06 05 04 03 02 01 00

10 9 8 7 6 5 4 3 2 1

To my husband,
who has always believed in me
more than I have believed in myself

Contents

Foreword

Effective church drama has an unbelievable ability to break down the
walls we have built in our hearts. Persons who may offer excuses following a convicting sermon or a stirring song often find themselves
forgetting those arguments and becoming intimately involved in a
well-presented dramatic scene. Somehow, the dialogue, costumes,
props, and actors join together to give us an intriguing look into
someone else's life. But in the course of the drama, we end up catch-
ing a glimpse of our own reality as well. We find ourselves relating to
the characters in the play. We laugh with them. We sympathize with
them. At times we even get angry with them. And as we do, we begin
to see ourselves in those personas. We begin to look more objectively
at our own life and at our relationship with God. As we become
engaged in the drama, we are given the opportunity to reevaluate our
own values and beliefs. This is the power of effective church drama.

The problem is that such dramas are hard to find. Many scripts
lack credibility. Some are so deep that you would need a degree in
philosophy just to make sense of them. Still others assume that the
director and actors are seasoned professionals. With these issues facing Christian churches, it is no wonder that many of them become
discouraged and abandon their drama ministry.

The answers to many of such churches' questions and solutions to
their problems can be found in the pages of this book. Author Laura
Martinez has not only provided well-written scripts, but she offers

clear directions for how to make the scripts work for your church, even with limited resources. In *Drama for the Dramatically Challenged,* you will be guided each step of the way. More than being just a collection of useable skits, it is a handbook on how to create effective church drama. May you use it to break down the walls of the heart as you build the kingdom of God.

Michelle Dawson
Assistant Professor of Communication
Spring Arbor College
Spring Arbor, Michigan

Preface

When I first decided to pursue publishing this work, I sought out a
friend who is a freelance journalist. She advised me to head to the
local library and check out a resource called *The Writer's Guide* in
order to get the addresses and editors' names for different Christian
publishing companies that might be interested in my proposal.
Because the information on each company was quite extensive,
rather than taking notes on each one, I decided to photocopy the
pages I needed. As I did so, I inadvertently copied a page I did not
need—or so I thought! As I was about to throw away the page, it
occurred to me that I should look at it first, just in case it contained
information that might be of some use. After all, the copy had cost
me a whole ten cents! I saw the name "Judson Press" and quickly
scanned the description under it. Seeing the word "Christian," I
decided to tuck the page into my folder and look at it more closely at
home. Several days later as I was preparing to send my book idea to
various Christian publishers, I mused, "Wouldn't it be funny if Judson
Press is the one who wants it! It sure would be obvious that Someone
is directing the publication of this book!"

Of course, Judson Press *was* the publisher to accept the book. I
sent out more than twenty letters and received several responses that
said, "This sounds great, but we don't do drama" or "Sorry, but we
just recently released a drama book." Only Judson responded with a
letter expressing interest: "Send us a sample and we'll talk."

Coincidence? Just "dumb luck"? I don't think so. Only my God could have arranged this one. I know because God has done it before.

I enrolled at Spring Arbor College in Spring Arbor, Michigan, and entered the communication department pursuing a major in speech and theater. After I successfully completed four years of preparation for a career in professional Christian drama, God led me into ten years of youth ministry! But God did not let my education go to waste. Instead, my training had prepared me for a different sort of dramatic career. Soon I was directing youth puppet teams and a clown troupe, producing Easter sunrise services, and directing the drama portions of adult musicals. When the right script for an occasion couldn't be found, I wrote one myself. If my creation went over well, I would occasionally think, "Maybe someday I'll publish that."

After leaving full-time youth ministry to be an at-home mom, I started a drama worship team at our church and continued writing sketches for various occasions. It was during that time that the dream of publishing truly began to take shape.

So, was studying theater and then entering youth ministry just a strange twist of fate, or was it divine intervention? Do I stumble through this life doing the best I can, or does God Almighty have a plan? I believe the latter is true. I would not say that I have never gotten off the beaten path or wandered from the divine plan, but God is good and always gets me back on track when I seek God's will.

> "Surely I know the plans I have for you, says the LORD, plans for your welfare and not for harm, to give you a future with hope" (Jeremiah 29:11, NRSV).

I pray that this book will help believers and nonbelievers alike to seek God and to follow God's plan for their lives.

Acknowledgments

All my love and gratitude go out to the following people, without whom this book may have never come into being: My Lord and Savior, Jesus Christ, from whom all talent, inspiration, and energy come. My husband, Joe, who has always encouraged me to go for my dreams and believed I could achieve them. My wonderfully dramatic son, Devon, who can make even me believe he's crying when he's really just acting! Dad and Mom, who have always supported me and even endured that annoying "answer the phone like a pizza place" phase. My brothers and sisters, who amazingly turned out to be really great people—I'm glad I didn't trade you in! My youth pastor, Steve Swope, who, without even knowing it, provided the vehicle for me to discover my talent for acting—a skit in an Easter sunrise service. My theater professor, Esther Maddox, who taught me as much about godly living as she did about theater. Dr. Thomas Bell, my communications professor, who graciously recorded the narration for "A Father's Love" on the companion CD. All my Spring Arbor College (SAC) instructors—thanks for being patient and for modeling Christ to me. Take Two, the SAC comedy and drama team—thanks for being so patient as I tried my hand at writing and directing. The members of the Elkton United Methodist Church and Wakeshma Community Church (WCC) youth groups, who patiently endured sunrise service rehearsals (among other things)—thanks for having made my life so much richer! The WCC drama worship team—thanks for helping me work the bugs out of the majority of these skits! The WCC congregation, who have been most gracious guinea pigs—thanks for all your encouraging comments, raucous laughter, and hearty applause. Dave and Michelle Dawson of Dawson Communications, who produced the compact disk that accompanies this book—your friendship and love have helped me more than you know. Dave also composed and performed all the music heard on the CD. Elizabeth Spencer, my writing guru—thank you for all your help, advice, and encouragement as I traveled the road to authorship. Tami Walker, Pam Waldron, Kathy McGlynn, and Mom, who provided countless hours of free baby-sitting so I could concentrate on finishing this book. Randy Frame, my editor—I still can't believe I can say that!—thanks for going to bat for me and believing in this project. Thanks to everyone at Judson Press for working with me on a dream come true!

Key to Symbols

The following symbols are found in the introduction under the heading "Director's Tips and Training" on page 7:

☞ **TIP:** Helpful advice and instruction for the director. These tips are intended to help you guide your actors in various theater skills.

↻ **TRAINING:** Exercises to help your actors learn a particular skill, such as vocal projection, or how to follow stage directions.

The next symbol is located throughout the various sketches:

👂 **SOUND EFFECT:** Indicates the appropriate place for a sound effect. The accompanying compact disk has all the sound effects you will need. (All sound effects are optional, to be used at your discretion.)

Introduction

DIRECTOR TO DIRECTOR

If you are not an experienced director, you may wish you could sit down and talk with one. If you have access to someone in the field of theater or know someone with "connections," it may be helpful for you to do just that. If you do not have the luxury of accessing a personal theater consultant, however, this introductory chapter should offer you some helpful insights.

Knowing the Lingo

You don't have to be a die-hard thespian to be able to use a script and stage effectively. Here are a few words and symbols you need to know. (For a more comprehensive list of theatrical terms, see the Glossary on page 121.)

Blocking. The movement of the actors to their various locations on the stage. A wise director does not wait for the first dry run to decide the blocking. This should be well thought out with detailed notes in the director's script. (But make your notes in pencil. Sometimes what works in theory doesn't in practice. Be flexible!) Plan your blocking with the audience in mind. If your audience can't see or hear what's going on, they will miss the message of the drama.

Stage business. The smaller movements of the actors that may or may not require them to change stage location. For instance, in "Burnt Cookies," Mom is in the kitchen making cookies and fixing dinner. As she speaks with the various members of her household who come into the kitchen, she should not just stand still waiting to deliver her next line. Even during dialogue she needs to appear busy by stirring batter, putting cookies in the oven, wiping the table, etc. This is called *business*.

Stage directions. Directions given to actors indicating their locations on the stage. These are often seen as capitalized initials such as DL and C. These may seem confusing at first, but understanding how these location names came about will help you remember them. In the early days of theater, the stages were slanted down toward the audience, not the other way around as we see today. Therefore, the front of the stage (closest to the audience) is known as downstage or D. The back of the stage (farthest from the audience) is called upstage or U. And the middle is center or C. Right (R) and left (L) are always the actor's right and left as he or she faces the audience. So the stage is divided into fifteen areas that look like this:

UR	URC	UC	ULC	UL
R	RC	C	LC	L
DR	DRC	DC	DLC	DL

Audience

This many stage areas are impractical for most church platforms or other small stage areas, however. In these cases a more simplified diagram is used:

UR	UC	UL
R	C	L
DR	DC	DL

Audience

The symbol *X* indicates a cross, or physically moving from one place on the stage to another. Therefore the stage direction "Bill DR X to UC" translates to "Bill, who is downstage right, crosses to upstage center." It is essential that all your players have a good understanding of these stage areas if you intend to use them in your directing. For a fun game that will help everyone get a handle on stage directions, see "Which Way Do I Go?" on page 11.

Actors' positions. The position of the actors' bodies in respect to the audience. These are rarely spelled out in a script but may be used by the director when blocking a scene. The main positions are listed below.

open: The actor's body faces toward the audience to some degree. For example, if the actor is standing at a 45-degree angle to the audience, he or she is *three-quarters open.* If there is no angle, it is called *full open.*

profile: The actor's body is at a 90-degree angle to the audience. This position is specified as *left profile* or *right profile.*

closed: The actor's body faces away from the audience. If there is no angle, we say the actor is in the *full closed* position. A 45-degree angle is *three-quarters closed.*

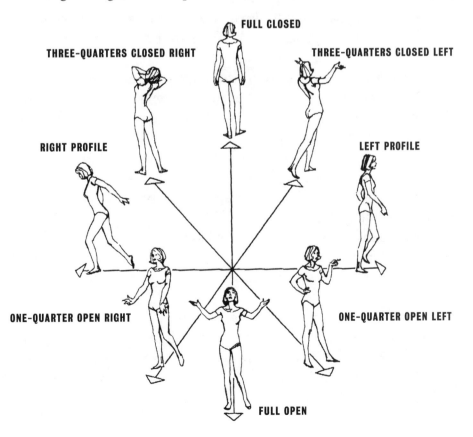

FULL CLOSED

THREE-QUARTERS CLOSED RIGHT

THREE-QUARTERS CLOSED LEFT

RIGHT PROFILE

LEFT PROFILE

ONE-QUARTER OPEN RIGHT

ONE-QUARTER OPEN LEFT

FULL OPEN

upstaging: One actor is farther upstage than another, forcing the downstage actor to turn away from the audience in a more closed position. There are a few occasions when this technique would be appropriate, but as a general rule, upstaging should be avoided because any lines the downstage actor needs to deliver to the upstaging actor will be spoken away from the audience, making the dialogue harder to hear.

cheating out: When two people talk in real life, they tend to face each other. However, it is preferable to have actors onstage stand at an angle to one another in a more open position, making them easier for the audience to see and hear. This so-called cheating out is often used during conversation between two or more players. An audience will overlook this not-quite-true-to-life aspect of the theater.

Trying to Do It All

If you are in the situation where you are lucky to get even a handful of people involved in your dramatic undertaking, you may find yourself playing a part as well as directing the piece. I learned the hard way how very taxing this can be. In college, each student in my theater production class had to direct a one-act play. I rounded up my four actors, conducted rehearsals, and found that I had a knack for directing. Things were going well. But then, only a few rehearsals before the performance, I lost my leading lady. There was no time to recast the part. I had no choice but to take it myself. I loved acting, so I figured I would simply combine it with my newfound love of directing and get the best of both worlds.

What I found was that directing became a terrible burden when I was acting in the same piece. Much directing needs to take place from the floor, where the director can watch the actors as they move about on the stage. It is very hard to watch for visual problems and listen for appropriate volume when you yourself are on the stage in the midst of the sketch. It is equally difficult to learn your lines and movements and create a smooth, natural appearance to them if you spend your rehearsals offstage watching the other actors. It can be very stressful!

I'm not saying it can't be done. My one-act came off fairly well. But I also learned a very valuable lesson: don't act in and direct the same piece unless it is absolutely necessary! Now, maybe you're saying, "But it is absolutely necessary." I understand. Here are a few tips to help make it a little easier.

1. Cast yourself in the least taxing part. Fill the bigger roles with your other actors and take a small one for yourself, preferably one that does not require your presence on the stage for very long.

2. Be on the stage with the others as you work out the blocking of the piece. Once they have a good idea of where you'll be when, get off the stage.

3. Have line rehearsals, where you simply rehearse lines without movement. This will enable you to put down your director's script and make sure you know your lines and cues well.

4. Set up a video camera on a tripod and tape your last two rehearsals. This way you can be on the stage as an actor and can watch the video later as the director. (Actually, it's not a bad idea to do this even if you're *not* acting. The video will help the other players to see what aspects of the performance need to be worked on.)

5. Enlist help with gathering props and finding costumes. This shifting of some of your other responsibilities will help you to avoid overload.

Leading with a Listening Ear

As you work on a piece, your players may have ideas and suggestions. Listen to them carefully. They may think of something you didn't. Let your actors know you value their input by asking for suggestions when you're not sure of the best way to do something. The elaborate blocking for "As Shepherds Watched Their Flocks" was a collaborative effort of my players and myself. When suggestions are made, don't be afraid to say, "I'm not sure if that will work. Let's run that scene again and try it." If it works, great. If it doesn't, politely let the actor know why it didn't. In the sketch just mentioned, one of my actors took many a tumble as we tried this or that. I watched from the floor and offered suggestions such as, "That looked good, but we need to get you turned around in time to run into Shepherd 3." It was great fun working together to come up with something both fun to do and to watch. All of us had a sense of ownership and wanted to make it the best we could at the performance.

With that said, you mustn't lose your sense of leadership when including your players in decisions. Some things need to be decided by you alone. You have a unique perspective the actors on the stage cannot share from their vantage point, and they need to trust your judgment. The basic blocking of a sketch is included in most scripts, but you may have to adapt it to your facilities. Unless there is a good reason for using a different door than the one you have designated for Actor B's entrance, you need not have a democratic vote on the subject. It is the director's job to make such decisions. It is also the director's prerogative to change the blocking if the original blocking is not working (although this should be done early in the rehearsals, not at the last minute if at all possible).

Walking and Talking

It is usually unwise to have a nonspeaking actor cross to a new stage location while another actor is delivering lines. This directs the audience's focus away from the speaking actor, since movement draws attention. The general rule is, "Cross on your own lines, not on someone else's." The more attention you want focused on the speaker, the less movement there should be on the stage. So in the case of a moving speech that gets to the heart of the piece, all other actors onstage should not even scratch an itch! But if a character says, "Jane, come here. You just have to see what I bought at the mall," Jane does not have to wait until the line is complete before moving but can walk toward the speaker as soon as she is summoned.

Why Discuss the Piece?

Discussion questions have been included after each sketch in this book for a number of reasons. One is that skits make a great discussion starter for youth groups and Bible studies. They provide a fun way to get our minds going so we can dig deeper into a subject. But from the perspective of a director, discussion questions are useful in helping your players grasp the meaning of the piece. Not only will they receive personal spiritual growth as they discuss the skit's theme, but they will also be better equipped to convey that meaning through their acting.

I remember a time in a college theater course when I was to participate in a scene for the class to observe. I was to play the part of a young woman who had straightened her hair and was getting a lecture from her brother about it. I had taken plenty of time to familiarize myself with the piece and felt prepared. But while we were in the midst of the presentation in class, my professor interrupted us. She was obviously upset and said she expected us to prepare before class. I was confused at her frustration. As she reprimanded us (and me in particular), it came out that the character I was playing was a young African American woman. Suddenly the whole piece changed. My lines had new meaning, and I was able to complete the scene to my professor's satisfaction. I had been missing a key part of the theme and had been unable to communicate that theme through my acting.

You will find your presentations to be much more meaningful for your audience as well as for your players if you set aside time to discuss the meaning of the piece after the first read-through.

DIRECTOR'S TIPS AND TRAINING

Anticipating Laughter

☞ Nothing is quite as encouraging as hearing an audience break out in laughter after a humorous line in a sketch. However, an unprepared player can break the flow of the piece or cause the audience to miss part (possibly a key part) of the dialogue. Prepare your players to anticipate laughter by noting where they laugh during a preliminary read-through of the sketch. Point out that when an audience laughs, the players need to stay in character (as if the audience were not there) and at the same time try to sense the crescendo of the laughter.

Beginning the next line of dialogue just as the laughter begins will cause many, if not most, of the audience to miss it. However, waiting too long to resume dialogue causes an awkward silence that shifts attention from the sketch to the players. While waiting for the laughter to die down a bit, actors should remain in character and attempt to keep the scene alive by using gestures and actions appropriate to their characters. Freezing the scene while waiting for laughter to subside is not an effective choice.

↻ Here is an exercise I've used with my drama team to help them in this area. Have two or three players improvise a scene for two minutes. Give them a setting, a situation, and a role for each person to enact (for example, a sunny day in the park, a grandmother and her five-year-old grandson are approached by a police officer wanting directions to the police station). Forewarn them that you will be laughing as they play out the scene and they are to gauge their pauses accordingly. As they improvise, break in with laughter at appropriate as well as inappropriate times. A little chuckle shouldn't interrupt the flow at all, but a loud, long laugh should cause the players to pause in their dialogue (but stay in character), until the laughter begins to decrescendo.

Being Heard

☞ We live in a wonderful world of technology. Microphones, especially lapel mikes, are wonderful things. Unfortunately, most of us do not have access to enough lapel mikes to make it a feasible way to ensure every line of dialogue is heard. Wireless mikes have to be held or put on stands, and corded mikes are accidents waiting to happen. While a few strategically placed microphones can be helpful, good, old-fashioned projecting is essential.

My theater professor always told us to imagine a deaf old lady in the back row. Everything we said on stage had to be heard by her–without shouting. This is a good rule of thumb for your players as well. It is a very rare thing that someone speaks too loudly while onstage. However, speaking too softly is frustratingly common.

↻ To help your players practice projecting their voices, use the improvisation exercise described above, but tell your group *you* are playing the deaf old lady in the back row. After you're seated comfortably in the back, allow the scene to begin. (You obviously need to be in a very large room for this to work. Try a sanctuary, gym, fellowship hall, etc.) If at any time the dialogue becomes the least bit hard to hear, stand up, cup your hand to your ear, and do your best old lady "Eh?" Encourage players to try a number of situations where volumes would naturally change: a heated argument, sharing something confidential, etc.

My Three Cardinal Rules of the Stage

☞ At every rehearsal where players are working from memory and before every performance, I can be heard to say the following, "Speak slowly, loudly, and clearly." As I say this, I overenunciate and speak in an annoyingly slow, clear voice. Those who have worked with me for a number of years often say it with me with that "Oh, please" look on their faces. But these three things cannot be overemphasized.

↻ Here's a fun exercise to help your players work on these three rules. After a sketch is well in hand–blocking and lines are down cold–have a lines-only rehearsal. Have actors stand on the stage without moving and simply say their lines. But have them do this slowly, loudly, and clearly to the degree of being ridiculous. If your players can keep from falling over with laughter, it is a great way to drive home this point and help prepare them to slow down for the actual performance. Very rarely does an actor deliver lines too slowly during a performance. More often than not, nerves cause the dialogue to be delivered too rapidly.

Memorizing Lines

☞ Having been in youth ministry for ten years, I have been guilty on many occasions of letting my students read lines off of scripts during a performance. Though we received compliments on our performances, they were surely not as impressive as they could have been. It is sometimes hard enough to get people (young or old) involved in theatrical undertakings, let alone interest them in a script that will require memorizing lines and learning cues. Whenever possible, however, insist on memorized lines. When memorizing is asking too much, there are some compromises and tricks you can employ.

There are times when allowing players to read a portion of their lines is workable. For instance, when a character is supposed to read a passage from a book, those lines can be taped inside a book and then be read rather than memorized. The temptation will be to place dialogue lines in the book as well. This is usually not a good idea.

Characters such as news anchors can have scripts on their anchor desks; reporters can carry clipboards or notepads; talk show hosts can have note cards. The danger here is that the players will bury themselves in the script and appear less than natural.

A trick I used when staging "The Jill Donapew Show" was to put the entire script on posterboard cue cards. I then decked out an adult staff member with a headset and used her as the floor manager of the TV studio. She signaled the sound technician to play theme music and introduced the host over a microphone. Then as the sketch began, she flipped the cue cards. The disadvantage was that the kids' eyes were basically all glued to the same spot on the front pew. But overall, it gave more of the live talk show feel to the performance.

The key to all of these techniques is not letting your players depend on written scripts. They should know the material so well that if somehow their clipboard came up missing or the pages were out of order, they could improvise and not throw everyone off. This requires several group rehearsals as well as each individual rehearsing many times out loud on his or her own.

↻ Try asking your players to put their scripts away and have them run through the sketch as best they can. Do this with only two rehearsals left before the performance and then again at the last rehearsal. This exercise will help them to become more familiar with the flow of the piece and help prepare them for possible problems during the actual presentation.

A memorized sketch is really ideal. It tends to be more professional and more effective in touching audiences with its point. When players do a poor job of memorizing, it can be a director's worst nightmare! Remind actors that they need to memorize not only their lines but also their cues, which means they must know the line or action that comes just before *their* line or action. It isn't enough to know that I say, "I'd like to see you try." I must know that first another character says, "Get out, or I'll throw you out."

Once lines are well in hand, this exercise will help to make them more concrete in players' minds. (My drama professor used to have us do this during the last week of rehearsals, and often we would do it the night of the performance in the dressing rooms.) Have players make sure scripts are safely out of sight—except for yours or a prompter's if you are in the sketch. Then simply run the lines at warp speed. No expression is necessary. You're going for speed and accuracy here (though you still need to be understood). Pick up cues as quickly as possible and finish the piece in record time. You or a prompter should keep track of any problem areas and alert players to them at the end so they can work on them. If you have time, speed rehearse the problem areas again.

Program Additions

Encourage your group's creativity and add a fun dimension to your presentation at the same time by having players invent commercials to be used before, after, or in the middle of a sketch. Commercials could be designed to make church announcements or to promote various aspects of the Christian life, such as prayer, witnessing, or fellowship. They could actually advertise Christianity itself by having a salvation message. Commercials can be 100 percent original or can be parodies of actual commercials on TV or radio. Various forms of staging can be used to present these commercial messages: live onstage presentations, over-the-sound-system "radio" announcements, or even videotaped advertisements shown on a TV large enough for all audience members to see.

The only exercise to help your group with this one is to have them try it a few times. Brainstorm current ads and jingles; then pick a topic and give it a try! This can be a lot of fun, and the creativity and enthusiasm of your group may surprise you.

Which Way Do I Go?

☞ Knowing stage-direction lingo can make directing easier, but only if your players know it too. To find a detailed explanation of stage directions, see "Knowing the Lingo," which begins on page 1. Make learning stage directions fun by using the games below.

↻ Explain to your group that you will use five general stage areas: stage left, stage right, upstage, downstage, and center stage. Everyone begins at center stage, and then you call out various other areas. As they are called, players race to those areas. At first, let everyone stay in the game. After they've gotten the hang of it, play a few elimination rounds in which the last person to get to the stage area is out. For an added twist, throw in a few positions (see the list on page 3) at random times. For instance, you might call, "Stage left; center stage, closed; downstage, three-quarters open."

↻ This second exercise is a version of Twister. (You could even make spinners!) Players take turns going to staging areas in the position you choose. For example, you may send Bob—down right, closed; then Sally—left center, cheat out. It is best to use the nine stage areas for this game (see page 2) instead of the five general areas above. You could even throw in exits and entrances: "Jim—exit up left." After players get the hang of it, put a five-second time limit in place. Anyone unable to get to the called location in the directed position within five seconds is out.

The End

☞ Without the luxury of a huge curtain closing or a sudden blackout at the end of a sketch, we are often at a loss as to how to end a scene. Yet for actors to simply leave the stage immediately after the last line is delivered can rob the audience of that final, crucial moment in which they absorb the full meaning of the piece. So after the last line is spoken, have all onstage actors freeze for a mental count of three. This freeze needs to be complete—no movement whatsoever. At the freeze, actors should count silently, "One thousand one, one thousand two, one thousand three," and then dissolve the scene by quietly exiting the stage area. This gives the audience a moment to reflect and provides a clear ending to the piece.

During rehearsals, do the mental count aloud so the actors can get a feel for it. This will aid them in being in sync with one another at the final performance. When you are nearing the end of rehearsals, cease vocalizing the count to allow players a chance to practice it without your help. Don't worry if one actor moves a second before the others. As long as it's not too quick, whoever moves first will start the dissolve of the scene, and the others should follow suit. (You could assign one actor to count and lead the dissolve of the scene, especially if your group is having a hard time with this or is freezing for too long a time.)

↻   Use this exercise to practice complete freezes and mental counting. At the beginning of a rehearsal, inform your players that you will be calling out, "Freeze!" at different times. When they hear this word, they are to freeze completely and mentally count, "One thousand one, one thousand two, one thousand three," and then resume what they were doing. Keep them apprised throughout the rehearsal as to their progress. You should be able to see a marked improvement after six or seven times.

For added fun (on your part, anyway) call out, "Freeze!" at a later rehearsal without any warning.

Readers' Theater

☞ At first glance, readers' theater may appear to be an easy way to do a dramatic presentation. There are no props or costumes—players usually (but not always) wear like clothing such as black skirts/slacks and white shirts. Lines are not memorized but are read from a folder—usually a small black ring binder. But this formal style of drama is more than meets the eye. It requires a great deal of concentration and may even take more rehearsal time than a memorized sketch.

In readers' theater, actors do not move about the stage as much as they would in a skit, and they *almost never* look at each other or audience members. Movements are planned and methodical, and eyes always look out and over the audience, down at the floor, or up to the ceiling, depending on the words being spoken. This can be especially hard for actors who are used to interacting on the stage.

If you've never seen or done readers' theater, you may be thinking it sounds dull at best. Actually, it can be very moving when done well. Audience members get caught up in the words and their imaginations fill in the blanks. I have seen readers' theater done so well that later I could swear there had been props and costumes. I had become so caught up in the script, my mind had created the scene!

Another aspect of readers' theater is the blending of voices. It is much like a musical choir in that a good blend of vocal pitches is needed. If all your readers are females with higher pitched speaking voices, your presentation will seem flat. But with a good mix of men and women with high, medium, and low voices, your performance will have a rich, moving quality. Of course, not every word is read in unison. Some are read solo; others in pairs, trios, etc. This is determined by the meaning and the mood of the words. A sentence may be broken into phrases that are read by various players. When this happens, it is very important that the flow and rhythm of the sentence are maintained. It is imperative that players rehearse the piece many times, both together and alone, to ensure a smooth reading. Though it will not be memorized, players should be so familiar with the piece that they can look away from their script without losing their place.

Movement is also determined by the words and usually only requires a few steps. Some pieces allow for gestures such as raising hands or even sitting down. Actors should not look like robots, but they also must avoid being too relaxed. Since this is not a natural form of acting, it is your job as the director to watch carefully during rehearsals and point out places where actors look too stiff or too relaxed. Allow your players to make suggestions regarding movement, but don't be afraid to let them know if it doesn't work to the benefit of the piece.

If this form of theater is completely foreign to you, you may want to call a local college with a drama department and ask if they are aware of any readers' theater performances that you might attend.

To help your players learn to read in unison, start with something simple, such as a familiar passage of Scripture (for example, Psalm 23). Assign each person a number and then number each verse, giving some verses two or more numbers indicating that more than one person will read these verses together. Label at least one verse "all." Distribute copies and have players read through the passage aloud. Be forewarned, the first reading will be rough! Now have players stand on the stage area—anywhere is fine. Instruct them to listen to one another. If they are late coming in on a unison verse, instruct them to simply pick up where the other reader or readers are so they don't break the rhythm. On the third reading, ask players to be attentive to the mood and feeling of the words and to read with appropriate volume and expression. (You may want to point out a few specific places.) Finally, add some movements and have actors note them on their photocopy. Include at least one hand motion or a few steps for each person. Some may even move in unison. Now try putting it all together, instructing actors to choose a spot on the back wall as their focal point when delivering lines.

Here is a sample idea for Psalm 23:4a. (Have Readers 1, 2, and 3 take one step together with each italicized word.)

> **READERS 1,2,3:** Yea, though I *walk* through the valley of the *shadow* of death,
>
> **READER 1:** I will fear no evil.

Notice the rhythm to the reading and the steps. The abrupt stop in movement draws attention to the solo words, "I will fear no evil."

You will find several readers' theater pieces in the sketches portion of this book (e.g., see "Words from the Cross" and "Words past the Tomb"). Remember, don't look at them as a shortcut to a presentation. Rehearse them thoroughly.

WORKING WITH WHAT YOU'VE GOT

Too Many Parts, Not Enough Players

Having too few players for the number of parts is not as big a problem as you may think. With a little ingenuity, you can make this problem an opportunity for creativity. Double, or even triple, roles—especially small ones. Ensure the actor will have time to make appropriate costume changes and, if possible, make his or her way to a stage entrance different than the one last exited.

Costume changes help the audience differentiate between characters being played by the same person. Be careful to choose changes that are quick and easy but very distinct. Hats, jackets, ties, and other large accessories are good. A wig can also work, but the player should practice getting it on quickly to ensure a smooth transition. Makeup, such as lipstick, is not recommended unless it is the player's last role and removal of the makeup will not be necessary until after the performance.

For a little added humor, have a male double in a female role. By removing a man's jacket and replacing it with a woman's hat, a large beaded necklace, a purse, and gloves, your dashing young man is transformed into a woman! Of course, the hard part is talking him into actually going through with this.

More Players than Parts

For most directors, having more players than parts is a dream come true. Most of us have to beg people to take part in a skit. But once word gets out that you're having more fun on the platform than the congregation is in the pews, you may find yourself in just such a dilemma. Simply add characters as "extras" using one of the ideas—or combination of ideas—below.

Have two or more players stroll through a scene at an appropriate time ad-libbing conversation.

Cast someone as a cameraperson in a news scene. Have the player give the "5, 4, 3, 2, 1" hand signals and cue the reporter to start his or her part. If you give this person a real video camera, you'll have instant footage of your presentation to enjoy with the cast later!

Cast a makeup artist who dabs an anchorperson with a powder puff and then dashes offstage as the newscast begins.

Purchase or make a take board. Have a player stand DC and begin the sketch with the words, "As Shepherds Watched Their Flocks [or whatever the title is], take 1," and then snap the board closed.

Create commercials about church announcements or biblical principles and use your extra players to present them. Use them before, after, or even *in* your skit. When inserting a commercial in a sketch, interrupt the dramatic action with, "We'll be back after these messages" (see "Program Additions" on page 10).

Be creative. Look at the setting and ask yourself, "What other people might we see in this scene?" Then add them! A script is not Scripture; you won't be struck by lightning if you alter it to fit your needs.

Nowhere to Hide

Some of us are spoiled with convenient doors leading to and from the stage area. Players wait in a side room (known as the *wings* in theater jargon) and enter at the appropriate time. Then they disappear neatly when their part is done. Others of us, however, are not so fortunate. Here are a few options that may help.

Make your own wings. Enlist help from someone with a bit of carpentry skill to make folding wooden dividers or frames of PVC pipe in sturdy stands. Then have someone skilled in sewing make curtains of dark, lightweight fabric that fasten around the top of the pipe. (Be sure the fabric is not see-through, and consider using Velcro for the fastening.) Actors wait for their entrances behind these portable wings. Remind your players that they must be extremely quiet and still when in the wings. Insist they practice this at no fewer than the last two rehearsals. They may find the urge to talk, laugh, move, etc., extremely hard to resist.

A more simple approach is to have the actors simply sit in the front row of the audience and enter and exit from there. This will give a less professional look, but it is functional. Even with this method though, actors should not talk to one another or move around while they are offstage. They need to see those front seats as "backstage," where they are expected to wait quietly for their cues and not distract the audience.

Along these same lines is the freeze method. Actors not on the stage stand on the floor to the left and right of the stage area, depending on which side they will be entering from. All stand with their backs to the audience and remain *completely* still. Any movement in these "wings" will divert audience attention away from the stage. There should be no movement whatsoever. Again, this is a technique that should be practiced during rehearsals. It is harder to do than one might think.

Need a Window?

An elaborate set is not usually possible for one sketch, but the *illusion* of a set is possible. A lightweight door in a frame of two-by-fours can create the illusion of outdoors and indoors as the actors use it for exits and entrances. Just be careful where you place it. The saying "You make a better door than a window" exists for a reason.

A window can be created by placing a large empty picture frame on an easel and then inconspicuously duct-taping a kitchen curtain to the inside. For "Burnt Cookies" I used this method and tied back the curtains so Mom could look out and see the carolers. The window was placed DR in a location where it was easily accessible by Mom but did not obstruct the audience's view.

Use Your Space

Most church sanctuaries have lots of options for staging in addition to the platform area. Look around and ask, "How can I use this space to stage this piece creatively?" Keep in mind that some churches frown on unusual uses of sanctuary fixtures and furniture, so be careful to clear all your creative ideas with the powers that be. It is not worth offending someone, or losing your privilege to share through drama again, just to perform one creatively staged piece.

Use platform steps to create different levels for readers when doing a readers' theater type presentation. Use the center aisle as an entrance and side aisles for dramatic exits. Deliver lines from the balcony. As long as the staging enhances the message and is okay with church protocol, don't be afraid to try it.

Our church baptismal is located high behind the platform. During a children's musical we used it to show our wise men "traversing afar" during the song about them. They left King Herod and exited stage R. A few moments later they were seen walking down the steps into the baptismal and then out the other side. Soon after, they reentered the stage through a door on stage L and found themselves greeting the baby Jesus!

Does Jesus Need a Beard?

I once saw an Easter musical that was very well done for a small church with limited resources. The set was quite impressive, the music was excellent, and the costumes were convincing. But there was one thing I just could not get past. Several of the characters—Pharisees, disciples—wore fake beards, and one even wore a longhaired wig! It was all I could do to take them seriously. Thankfully, the man playing Jesus really had long hair, so he was not forced to wear a wig.

I'm all for trying to portray historical drama in authentic costume, but typically fake beards and wigs do not add to the drama; they detract from it. If the performance is meant to be serious, these additions defeat the purpose. It is hard to take Jesus seriously at the Last Supper when the actor portraying him has a wild clump of fake hair on his head.

An audience understands that this is a *performance,* a portrayal of an event and not the actual event itself. They will allow for Jesus having short hair, curly hair, or even red hair and no beard at all (although an unusual hairstyle or color may take a few moments to get used to at first). If the performance is good—script, acting, etc.—the audience will allow for these little "discrepancies" in their preconceived ideas about Jesus' appearance. But putting fake hair on actors becomes laughable and hard to dismiss.

What about a drawn-on beard using stage makeup? If you have someone who's good at using makeup in this way and if your audience will not be close enough to recognize it as makeup, then this may be an option. Of course, this will make for the appearance of a close-cut beard or even five-o'clock shadow, so if it's not essential to the script, you may be better off to forgo this addition.

What about Glasses?

Good question. As far as basic skits are concerned, glasses are usually fine. If the role is a biblical character, I strongly recommend avoiding glasses if at all possible. Although, as stated above, an audience realizes that this is only a portrayal of an event and thus they will make some allowances for actors' appearances, glasses are more difficult to overlook. For one thing, putting glasses together with historical costumes mixes modern accessories with ancient dress and can distract from the credibility of a serious dramatic piece. (In the case of a comedy, however, the mix may actually help!) Glasses may also reflect the glare of stage lights and can be distracting in the same way that other articles of jewelry can be. An actor with only moderately poor vision who does not wear contact lenses may be able to learn to maneuver around the stage with blurred vision. (Always have the actor rehearse without glasses if that is the way the actual sketch will be performed.) Sometimes you will have no choice, and an actor will have to wear glasses regardless of what that anachronistic detail does to the costume's authenticity. It is better if that person does not have to be lead character, however. Sometimes, for the sake of ensuring the most effective performance possible, a director has to make those types of difficult decisions based on an actor's height, age, or other physical trait; I myself did not get the lead role in a college production because I was too tall for the part.

As long as we're on the subject of accessories such as glasses, let me add that all jewelry should be removed when historical costumes are worn. It is not very convincing when Jesus comes out wearing a biblical costume and a sports watch! One exception is wedding rings. Depending upon the actor's skin tone, rings can be disguised by wrapping them with a small adhesive bandage or piece of tape of similar skin color.

Quick Fixes

It's bound to happen sooner or later. Your drama is about to begin when you discover Susie's costume hem is too long and she's sure to trip on it. Sewing is not an option. Fear not! A stapler or some duct tape will provide a quick fix. Duct tape is good for all kinds of last-minute disasters—broken props, falling set pieces, almost anything. Always have it on hand and don't be afraid to use it! Having extra safety pins on hand is a good idea too.

Useful Stuff

If you have the storage space and the resources, the following make versatile set pieces: stools, two-foot stepladders, and small folding chairs (all wooden). It is preferable to leave them in their natural wood rather than to paint them. Something about these pieces lends them to any purpose. Three wooden folding chairs become a believable sofa; two become the front seat of a car. Stools are great for narrators or can be effectively used in readings. Ladders can serve as seats that are easily moved and also allow readers to perform on various levels. If you are able to choose only one of the above, I recommend the ladders. They are more versatile than the other two options, and standing on folding chairs or stools can give new meaning to the theater adage "Break a leg"!

Involving Those Who "Don't Do Drama"

There are lots of places in a drama ministry for those who are not into acting. Use people in the following positions, or combinations of these positions, to reduce your stress and responsibilities:

properties manager: Gathers all needed props and makes sure they are where they need to be for rehearsals and performances. Is responsible for storing them when not in use.

costume manager: Gathers all costumes (or makes them, if he or she has the skill and time to do so). Oversees their care and storage.

stage manager: Moves set pieces on the stage for a performance and then off again when the skit is done. Works with properties manager in placing props. In the case of several set pieces, the stage manager coordinates the actors' help in clearing the stage quickly after a skit is performed.

director's assistant: Prompts actors when lines are forgotten during rehearsals. Sits beside director and takes notes as the director gives them during a rehearsal. (This allows you to keep your eyes and ears on the action at all times.) Stands in for an absent actor, reading his or her part during a rehearsal. Reminds actors of rehearsal times and any other pertinent information.

If someone has a heart to serve God and wants to be involved in your dramatic undertaking, do your best to find a place for that person. Having support people in the positions described above will make your job as director easier and more fun, and you may unknowingly help someone develop a God-given gift at the same time!

ABOUT REHEARSALS

How you run your rehearsals will be determined by the purpose of your group. If you are a youth minister preparing a skit for an Easter sunrise service, you will spend less time on training and more time on rehearsing. If you are beginning a drama ministry, training and rehearsing need to be on equal ground. Below are some of the components that make up one of my drama worship team rehearsals, followed by a sample rehearsal schedule.

Devotions

It's important not to forget what sets Christian drama apart from other types of drama. Our purpose is not simply to entertain but also to cause people to reflect on God—who God is and who he has called us to be. Taking time to focus on God and his Word at the beginning of a rehearsal helps everyone to keep the proper perspective.

If yours is a drama ministry team like mine, you may wish to focus your devotional time on a topic such as service, ministry, or worship. I have used excerpts from David Needham's book *Close to His Majesty* at our rehearsals because it has a wonderful chapter on worship. A devotional study guide on one of the above-mentioned topics (available at your local Christian bookstore) could be broken into bite-size chunks for a short devotional time.

If you are rehearsing for a one-time event, such as a Christmas program or youth rally, don't skip devotions. Again, for the sake of focus, this is an important element. Instead of taking on one of the broad topics above, stay focused on the theme of the skit itself. One suggestion would be to have the group read through the skit out loud (don't worry about assigning permanent parts; just pick someone for each one and go) and then do the discussion questions at the end of the piece. Follow up with a related Bible passage.

Exercises

Exercises can take on two forms: devotional and dramatic. Devotional exercises are related to the devotion topic. For example, as my group studies worship, we use exercises that will stretch us in our understanding of what it means to worship. Dramatic exercises are used to get creativity flowing and to loosen everyone up. Here are some ideas for each exercise category. Additional dramatic exercises appear in "Director's Tips and Training" on pages 7–14.

Devotional Exercises (for Topic of Worship)

1. Have group members form teams of two or three players. Then give them two minutes to write down every word they can think of that starts with W and has something to do with worship. These can include things related to a worship service, how we worship, what worship is, the one we worship, etc. At the end of the two minutes, call time and then rotate through the teams having each team take a turn sharing one of its answers. No answers may be repeated, so if team 1 says, "Wonderful," and team 2 had written that answer also, team 2 must cross it off and cannot use it. When a team has used all its answers, it is out. If an answer seems "way out," the other teams may challenge. Then the team with the questionable response must give an explanation for the answer. As the director, you are the final judge. If you feel the answer is unacceptable, then the team must cross it off and choose another answer. If the team doesn't have any more, then it is out. You'll be amazed at the variety of answers and insights! This exercise can also give you seven rehearsals' worth of exercises if you use a different letter from the word *worship* each week.

2. This next exercise is similar, and so it should be used instead of, or before, the one above. Again, divide into teams and give each team a piece of paper and a marker. Have them write the letters spelling "worship" down the left-hand margin of the paper. Then give them five minutes to come up with a word related to worship for each letter. (For added difficulty, narrow the field by limiting answers to a specific aspect of the topic, such as a worship service or the One we worship.) Caution players to come up with unique answers, since any duplicated by other teams will be eliminated, and remind them that they may choose only one answer per letter. After five minutes, have teams share their answers. All teams should cross off duplicate answers, including the one sharing the answer. Questionable answers can be challenged as above.

3. The next exercise should be assigned as homework the week before. Instruct players to locate a verse in the Bible that describes a position of worship (for example, kneeling). Be very clear that the verse must speak of worship, not prayer or something else, and that they must come prepared to read it and do it. At your next rehearsal, have members go to the platform or stage area one at a time and read the selected Scripture and then assume that position. When the first player has done so, he or she should freeze in that position as the second player comes on and reads. This continues until all players are on the stage in a position of worship. Then begin a quiet worship song, read a Scripture, or lead a prayer. Keep it short since the first players may be getting stiff at this point. Afterwards, have players sit comfortably on the stage. Ask them for insights. What was similar about the positions? Different? How did they feel?

4. Ask players to spend some time during the week finding a Scripture passage that causes them to be in awe of God. Encourage them to take some time with this and then meditate on the passage they choose. At the next rehearsal have each player share the chosen Scripture and talk for a few minutes about what it means to him or her.

Dramatic Exercises

1. Nursery rhymes make fun exercises. Have members choose a nursery rhyme to which they know all the words. Then have members take turns reciting their rhymes. Here's the catch: just before a member recites, you give that person an emotional direction in which to perform. For instance, a player may choose "Mary Had a Little Lamb," and you instruct her to perform it laughingly. The player must then recite the rhyme as if it is the funniest thing she's ever heard. Players may not, however, alter any of the words or add any words of their own. Other emotional directions could include angrily, sorrowfully, shyly, enthusiastically, and snobbishly.

2. The above exercise concentrates on use of the voice; this next exercise will focus on use of the body. Place a large, empty box on the floor; then hand out slips of paper with a type of person written on each. Players should not show anyone their assigned role. One at a time, players should approach the box, pick it up, and carry it to a new location. They must do this in a manner consistent with the role assigned. No talking is allowed, and no props may be used other than the box. For instance, a player assigned the role of "bodybuilder" may saunter up to the box, squat down, and lift it as if it were heavy but quite manageable by someone so strong. (This is especially fun if the player assigned this role is a petite female!) Because this exercise can play on stereotypes, be careful what roles you assign. Here are some additional suggestions: waiter, woman holding the hand of a small child, elderly person with a cane, an egghead, a three-year-old.

3. When I was in college, we sometimes played a game we called Enter and Alter. Two players begin a scene of their choosing. They dialogue and interact until another player sees an opportunity to alter the scene. That player says, "Freeze!" Action onstage immediately freezes, and the new player enters the scene replacing the player of his or her choice. Here's an example. The first two players are role-playing a scene at an ATM. The first player is having a bit of trouble with the machine, while the other waits impatiently. Suddenly the second player takes out a gun (his hand) and puts it in the first player's back. The first player's hands immediately shoot up in the air. Someone yells, "Freeze!" and then enters the scene. She replaces the first player, but instead of assuming his position with hands up, she faces the other player whose finger is pointing out like a gun. She then unfreezes the scene by pretending to open a door and saying, "If you kids don't stop ringing that doorbell! Oh, I'm sorry; it's you. Please come in." The second player must then adjust his role to play along with this new scene.

Again, at an opportune time, someone in the audience yells, "Freeze!" and then enters and alters the scene. You may want to apply the "longest player" rule to avoid one person being in every scene. The longest player rule says that when a new person enters the scene, he or she must replace the player who has been in the scene the longest. The newcomer may not replace the player who entered the scene last.

If you are having trouble getting everyone involved, assign each person a number, and you take over calling, "Freeze." Stop the scene every two minutes, give the next person a moment to think, and then have her enter and alter the scene. Don't leave yourself out. Set an example by being the first to jump in and try. This game can be a lot of fun, and you'll have to predetermine how long you'll play and then keep an eye on the clock.

Rehearsing

Assuming you have more than one rehearsal to prepare a sketch—and you really should if you want it to be polished and to pack a punch—you may wish to use the following outline when rehearsing.

1. Read through the sketch with players sitting comfortably. Talk through any possible problem areas. Use discussion questions to help everyone understand the theme of the piece. Assign parts.

2. Walk through the sketch having players read from the script and move about on the stage at appropriate times. (You should have already thought this through before the rehearsal. This is called blocking the scene. Be flexible, though. Sometimes what works in your head doesn't work on the stage.) Work out anything that isn't quite right.

3. Allow players to walk through the piece again, but this time you should sit and watch from the audience's vantage point. Interrupt as you observe things that need changing or attention.

4. Have players do a walk-through a third time, but this time without any interruption from you. Instead, you should take notes on anything you observe. For instance, your notes may read: "Becky—speak louder; Matt—cheat out; Juan—don't walk on Dexter's lines." Then go over the notes after the walk-through is done. Be sure to include positive notes as well, for example, "Aisha—good projection!"

5. At your next rehearsal, you may want to redo numbers 3 and 4 first. Then have the players put down their scripts and try it from memory. (Of course, you warned them sternly the week before that scripts must be memorized by this rehearsal!) During this first try without scripts, take notes and refrain from interrupting except to prompt forgotten lines. Share any observations you made.

6. Have players enact the scene again, but interrupt to correct problems with blocking, body use, vocal inflection, etc. (Try not to get too carried away. This isn't Broadway, after all.)

7. From here on out, you should not interrupt unless it is absolutely necessary. Take notes and go over them after the sketch is done. Work on any trouble sections, but always end with a beginning-to-end-no-interruptions run-through. Again,

remember not to be stingy with praise. Find the good stuff in every player and let them hear it!

8. A brief run-through just before your performance is a good idea, especially if it has been a few days since your last rehearsal. My group usually meets between Sunday school and the worship service to rehearse lines only. If time is short, we do a speed rehearsal (see "Memorizing Lines" on page 9). Then I give the players a pep talk and remind them of what we are trying to communicate through the piece. We wrap up with prayer and then wait nervously to share with the congregation.

Homework

I almost always assign some form of homework at the end of rehearsal. Keep in mind that your players are busy people with plenty of demands on their time. If you are sending them home saying, "This sketch needs to be memorized by next week," then don't assign any other task if at all possible. Other homework assignments could include gathering one's props and costume for the piece, preparing for the next week's devotional exercise, or finding a Scripture verse that applies to the theme of the sketch you are working on.

Sample Rehearsal Schedule

Below is a typical drama worship team rehearsal at my church.

6:30   Prayer and devotions

6:45   Devotional or dramatic exercise

6:55   Business—dates of upcoming dramas, etc.

7:05   Rehearse sketch (usually we are working on more than one at a time)

7:55   Wrap-up—reminders of homework, schedule, etc.

8:00   Dismiss

As Shepherds Watched Their Flocks

THEME: The excuses we use for not accepting Christ are unfounded and pathetic.

SETTING: The night of Christ's birth on a hill outside of Bethlehem

CHARACTERS: Four shepherds (Shep1, Shep2, Shep3, Shep4), three narrators (Nar1, Nar2, Nar3). All parts may be played by either males or females, although it would be preferable to have at least two male shepherds.

COSTUMES: Narrators can be dressed in street clothes, church clothes, white shirts and black pants/skirts, or white robes to give the illusion of angels. Shepherds can be dressed in authentic-looking costumes or in bathrobes, but do not try to combine bathrobes and authentic costumes.

PROPS: Four shepherd staffs (Tall thin branches are more convincing than the candy-cane staffs.)

[♪ 1–*optional music*]

NAR1: "And there were shepherds living out in the fields nearby, keeping watch over their flocks at night. An angel of the Lord appeared to them, and the glory of the Lord shone around them, and they were terrified. But the angel said to them, 'Do not be afraid. I bring you good news of great joy that will be for all the people. Today in the town of David a Savior has been born to you; he is Christ the Lord. This will be a sign to you: You will find a baby wrapped in strips of cloth and lying in a manger.'"

[𝄞 2–Nighttime sounds]

NAR2: It's dark; late at night. A hill. Sheep all around. Some sleeping, some eating. Shepherds keeping watch. Some standing in pairs talking quietly, some scanning the flock for signs of danger, some just fighting off sleep the best they can. Suddenly . . .

[𝄞 3–Musical sounder]

NAR3: Crash! Bang! Boom! Incredibly bright light. A huge, gorgeous, winged creature that has seemingly come out of nowhere hangs in the sky.

NAR1: Fear not!

NAR3: The words echo and resound off of everything–the hills, the sheep, the shepherds. They can feel it resonate in their chests.

NAR2: The angel's

NAR1: "Fear not!"

NAR2: doesn't go very far. The shepherds are terrified. What they were seeing and hearing at that moment was so foreign, so unbelievable, they could not have imagined it in their wildest dreams.

NAR3: The angel manages to focus their attention on the words and tells them all about the Christ child–where he is, how they'll know they have found him. After that, it's as if the lights of a thousand stadiums were all turned on at once in one place.

NAR1,2: Hundreds

NAR2: maybe

NAR1,2,3: thousands of angels

NAR2: filled the sky and sang praise to God.

NAR1: Unbelievable.

NAR3: And then, as if someone threw the breaker controlling the stadium lights, it was over. Darkness of night returned. Total silence.

NAR1: Then slowly a few crickets dared to chirp.

[𝄞 4–Night sounds with lamb bleating]

NAR2: A little lamb let out a halfhearted bleat, and then another.

NAR3: The shepherds began to come to.

[Lights come up on shepherds, who are staring off toward right upper corner]

SHEP3: *[Mouths "wow," taps Shep2, and starts moving L]* Come on! Let's go! *[Realizes the others are frozen, X R]* Yoo-hoo!

[Suddenly they snap out of their trances. There is chaos as they run around dropping and retrieving their staffs and running into each other. As they run around, they are saying things such as "Oh man," "Hurry up," "An angel!" etc. During all of this, Shep3 X L and watches, shaking head. Finally all are in line beside Shep3 fixing headwear, etc.]

SHEP3: *[Calmly]* Ready?

SHEP2: All set!

SHEP1: Yep, let's go!

SHEP4: *[Wanders DC]* I don't know. Maybe we shouldn't leave right away. I mean, the angels didn't give us an exact time. Maybe we should wait 'til morning.

SHEP3: What?!

SHEP4: We've got plenty of time. That baby's not gonna grow up over night. Besides, what are we gonna tell the sheep?

SHEP3: *[Exasperated]* Oh come on.

SHEP1: *[Moving toward Shep4]* Wait a minute, guys; maybe he's right.

SHEP3: What do you mean, maybe he's . . .

SHEP1: Now, hang on. I'm only thinking of the baby's mom. Maybe she won't want visitors, and especially not stinky, grimy shepherds.

SHEP4: Yeah, we are all smelling a little like sheep—or hadn't you noticed?

[Shep2 does a quick armpit sniff and reacts as if it's pretty bad]

SHEP1: Let's clean up first; then we can go see the baby.

SHEP2: *[Moves toward others]* Now that you mention it . . .

SHEP3: Not you too!

SHEP2: Well, think about it. Maybe that whole angel thing was just a mirage.

SHEP3: What?!

SHEP2: *[Convincing self]* Yeah, a figment of our imaginations. *[To Shep3]* Come on, you don't really believe in that angel stuff; do you?

SHEP1: You know, we have been out here with these sheep a long time. Maybe we've finally lost our grip on reality.

SHEP4: Or maybe we just conjured this up to give ourselves a sense of significance.

[Shep1, Shep2, and Shep4 nod in knowing agreement]

SHEP3: But we just . . . *[Giving up and then trying again]* . . . with our own eyes . . . *[Looks defeated–pause]* Great! Just great! All right, you guys do what you want. I'm going to see this baby . . . tonight . . . just like I am. *[Shep3 storms off L]*

SHEP4: He's such a radical! *[X DR to original position]*

SHEP2: Well, I guess some people just have to learn the hard way. *[Shep2 and Shep1 X DR to original positions]*

[All freeze staring out R and down]

[⌒ 5–Background music]

NAR1: "When the angels went away from them into heaven, the shepherds said to one another, 'Let us go over to Bethlehem and see this thing that has happened, which the Lord has made known to us.' And they went with haste, and found Mary and Joseph, and the babe lying in a manger."

NAR2: The most amazing part of the whole story is not the angel with the bright lights and booming voice. It's not the troops that joined him later. It's not even the fact that the shepherds didn't die of pure fright.

NAR3: No, the amazing part is the phrase,

ALL: "And they went."

NAR3: What if that had been you and I on that hill? Would we have hurried to the manger?

NAR1: The Bible says they went with haste. That means they didn't waste any time.

NAR2: Or would we have stood around making excuses that kept us from going to meet God?

NAR1: I'm not good enough. I'll clean up my act first, and then God will accept me.

NAR2: I have other things to do right now; I'll think about God later.

NAR3: God? God's just somebody that people of ancient times dreamed up—a figment of the imagination designed to make us feel better or keep us in line.

NAR2: God's too busy to be bothered with insignificant little me.

NAR1: "When the angels went away from them into heaven, the shepherds said to one another, 'Let us go over to Bethlehem and see this thing that has happened, which the Lord has made known to us.'"

NAR3: "And they went with haste, and found Mary and Joseph, and the babe lying in a manger."

ALL: "And they went."

NAR1: Will you?

NOTE: Scriptures are quoted in the following order: Luke 2:8–12 (NIV), 15–16 (NRSV).

Alterations

Shorten this script and reduce the number of players needed by deleting the narration. Simply begin with someone introducing the sketch by saying something like this: "Most of us are familiar with the biblical account of the shepherds receiving the news of Christ's birth. We know they heard the news and headed to Bethlehem. But what if it had been you and I on that hill watching our flock? How might we have responded to the angel's news?"

Hints

Be creative when blocking the "chaos" part of the sketch. Allow players to give input and use any special tumbling talents someone may have. We blocked it bit by bit and went through the total scene in slow motion each time we added a new component. Below is our beginning placement of the four shepherds followed by a description of our version of the "chaos."

DR—front row on bent knee from stage R to L: Shep2, Shep3; back row standing from R to L: Shep4, Shep1.

After Shep3's "Yoo-hoo," Shep1 reaches down and helps Shep2 up by the arm, causing them to face one another. They run into each other, then spin in opposite directions. Shep1 drops his staff near C and falls on all fours to retrieve it. Meanwhile Shep4 and Shep2 have run into each other, causing Shep4 to drop her staff and begin to retrieve it as Shep2 spins around and heads toward C only to trip over Shep1, who is retrieving his staff. Shep2 drops her staff and does a somersault as she flips over Shep1, who then gets up, staff in hand, and begins to X L. Shep2 gets up and runs R only to be knocked onto her back when Shep1 collides with her. During the acrobatics, Shep4 has been running L, R, L, R, in a confused manner (keeping R of the action at C.) She now crosses to C and extends a hand to help Shep2 up as Shep1 helps Shep2 up from behind and then spins her around to face Shep3 standing at stage L. (Shep1 remains behind Shep2 during this spin.) As they spin, Shep4 retrieves Shep2's staff, and they all run L with Shep2 running into Shep3, then Shep1 into Shep2, and so on in a sort of reverse domino effect.

The above blocking requires a lot of practice to make it look realistic, but the effect is hilarious!

Discussion Questions

1. What kinds of excuses do people make when confronted with the need to accept Christ as their Savior? Give examples of excuses you have heard.

2. Are any of these excuses legitimate? Why or why not?

3. What excuses, if any, have you used?

4. Come up with responses to each of the above excuses.

5. Why do you think people make excuses like these?

Burnt Cookies

THEME: Many Christians offer only lip service at Christmastime, saying they believe that "Jesus is the reason for the season" but often living quite something else.

SETTING: The kitchen on a Sunday evening just before the annual Sunday school Christmas program.

CHARACTERS: Mom, Mel (a child about six years old, either girl or boy), two kids (preferably boys) about nine and ten years old (Kid1, Kid2), Dad, group of carolers (two with speaking parts: Caroler1, Caroler2).

COSTUMES: Everyday clothes with these additions: Mom—apron; Dad—coat; kids—coats, mittens, and at least one knit hat; Mel—large bed sheet (mostly white but should have some design), safety pins, duct tape or clothes pins (used to keep the sheet on), wire coat hanger wrapped with Christmas garland (for a tacky halo), wings; carolers—coats, hats, mittens.

PROPS: Table with bowls, spoons, dish towel, four cookie sheets, oven mitts; "oven," perhaps crafted from a cardboard box; something resembling a window that Mom can look through DR, if possible; two sleds filled with paper snowballs; paper shopping bag with the name of a predominantly men's store in large letters (e.g., Lowe's, Home Depot, or even a fabricated name, such as ABC Hardware); four dozen burnt cookies, real or fake (we used chocolate no-bake cookies); nonfolding chair or kitchen stool (should make Mel taller than Mom when standing on it).

(From Laura L. Martinez, *Drama for the Dramatically Challenged: Church Plays Made Easy* © 2000 by Judson Press. Reproduced by permission.)

[The first batch of cookies is already in the oven]

MOM: *[Already a bit frazzled]* OK, three dozen cookies, get supper on, finish Mel's angel costume, and . . . anything else? Oh yes, and remember–Jesus is the reason for the season. *[Exaggerated smile]*

MEL: *[Enters from UL]* Mom, when are you gonna do my costume?

MOM: Soon dear. I have to finish these cookies for the afterglow tonight.

MEL: Why do they call it an afterglow?

MOM: Um, well, it's after the program, and, uh, well . . . *[With confidence]* we'll all be glowing with pride because of the great job you all did in the Sunday school program.

MEL: Oh.

[Mom stirs something on the table]

MEL: Something smells funny.

MOM: My cookies! *[Hurries to retrieve them but is too late–they're burned]*

MEL: What about my costume?

MOM: In a minute, dear. Go practice your part.

MEL: OK. *[Exits UL]*

MOM: *[With less feeling than before]* Jesus is the reason for the season. *[Deep breath, tries harder]* Jesus is the reason for the season. *[Weak smile, starts putting more cookie dough on a new cookie sheet, puts it in the oven when finished]*

[Arguing starts in the back of the audience. Kid1 and Kid2 come down the center aisle in a heated battle, dragging sleds filled with paper snowballs, with which they try to pelt each other throughout their walk to the front, but each always ducks in time to make sure an audience member is the actual recipient of the snowball (throw softly!).]

KID1: I was king on the mountain way longer than you were.

KID2: Were not.

KID1: Was too.

KID2: Were not.

KID1: Was too.

KID2: You're so stupid, a two-year-old's smarter than you.

KID1: Is not.

KID2: Is too.

KID1: Is not.

KID2: Is too.

KID1: Oh yeah? Well you're so ugly, everybody thinks you're wearing a Halloween mask all the time!

KID2: Do not.

KID1: Do too.

[By now the kids should be entering the DL door and then coming onstage through the UL door (without the sleds)—the argument continues loudly even as they disappear. As they enter UL, Kid1 gets in a last "do too" and pulls Kid2's hat down over his eyes and makes a run for it. A chase around the kitchen table—and Mom—ensues with Mom saying things such as, "Boys," "Stop this," etc.]

MOM: *[With gusto]* Enough!

[Boys stop immediately, hopefully R of Mom]

MOM: We have an hour and a half before we leave for the church. You were supposed to be home an hour ago. Now march upstairs and get ready.

[Boys begin to head UR, pushing and shoving with a few more quiet "do not, do too"s]

MOM: Do you know your parts?

[Boys stand shoulder to shoulder looking as angelic as possible]

KID1: And he shall be called Wonderful,

KID2: Counselor,

KID1: the Mighty God,

KID2: the Everlasting Father,

BOTH: the Prince of Peace! *[Heads together with cheesy grins for this last line; then they race out pushing and shoving. Kid2 leans back in to deliver next line, then disappears.]*

KID2: Do you smell something?

MOM: My cookies! *[As she retrieves them, she fans imaginary smoke. With no energy]* Jesus is the reason for the season. *[No smile]*

[Mel enters UL dressed in a sheet that looks like a six-year-old rigged it up. She has a makeshift halo sitting crooked on her head.]

MEL: Mom, listen to me say my part.

[Mom is starting another batch of cookies]

MEL: *[Stands on a chair or kitchen stool]* "As shepherds washed their flocks at night, Lou, the angel of the Lord, appeared." *[Pause]* Mom, I thought the Christmas angel was named Gabriel.

MOM: Yes, I think that's right.

MEL: Uh-uh, his name is Lou.

MOM: What?

MEL: "Lou, the angel of the Lord, appeared."

MOM: Lo, honey. And, lo, the angel of the Lord appeared. *[Puts cookies in oven]*

MEL: Oh. And, LO, *[Uses deepest six-year-old voice]* the angel of the Lord appeared. And they were sore afraid. *[Thinks again]* Can you imagine being so scared it hurt?

MOM: *[Starts to explain]* Well actually, honey, that means . . . uh no, I can't. Keep going.

[🔊 6–knock]

[Carolers should make their way down the left audience aisle as quietly as possible and "knock" at an imaginary door DR before Mel can continue. Mom sighs, looks out the "window."]

MOM: Oh no, carolers.

MEL: What are carolers?

MOM: Right now? A necessary holiday interruption.

[They go to the imaginary door and "open" it. Carolers sing a horribly off-tune carol.]

MOM: That was just lovely.

MEL: No it wasn't.

[Mom pulls halo down over Mel's mouth to gag her]

MOM: Let me give you a little something. *[Goes to the kitchen, looks around frantically, grabs a sheet of burned cookies, and hurries back. While she's gone, Mel frees herself from her gag.]*

MEL: *[With pride, as if it's good]* My mom says you're a necessary holiday interruption!

MOM: *[Appalled, quickly steps in front of Mel to offer the cookies]* Here you are.

[Carolers accept them reluctantly with weak "thank you"s and leave down center aisle. As they are walking, they are heard saying]

CAROLER1: You're not going to eat that, are you?

CAROLER2: *[Has taken off a mitten]* No, I'm putting it in my mitten to warm up my hand.

CAROLER1: Good idea!

[All the carolers start to do the same. By now Mom and Mel are in the kitchen again.]

MEL: Something smells like smoke. *[She scurries off UL]*

MOM: No. *[Almost in tears as she takes them out]* This is supposed to be a no-burn cookie sheet. *[Pauses for a moment; then, with much effort]* Jesus-is-the-reason-for-the-season. *[Picks up another full cookie sheet and puts it in the oven]*

[Dad has come quietly down right aisle during the last few lines, enters DL door and then UL door on to the stage as he cheerfully sings a Christmas song. He is carrying a shopping bag turned so the audience can clearly read it.]

MOM: Where have you been? We have to leave in an hour.

DAD: I'm sorry, but when I'm out shopping for my best girl, I want to take my time and find just the right gift.

MOM: *[Glances at the bag]* Mmhm. Well, wash up and call the kids so we can eat.

DAD: Eat. Oh, that reminds me, tomorrow is the staff Christmas potluck at work. I need a dish to pass and a dozen cookies. *[Glances at last batch of burnt cookies]* Uhhh . . . how 'bout I save you a little time and pick up the cookies at the store.

MOM: You're too kind.

DAD: *[X UR]* Always thinkin' of you, hon. *[Starts to exit, leans back in and sniffs a few times, shrugs. Mom throws an oven mitt at him. He exits. Mom is retrieving the cookies when Mel enters with wings added to her "costume"; they are very crooked.]*

MEL: Look, Mom, I finished my costume all by myself. *[Twirls]* Listen to the rest of my part, Mom. *[♪ 7–optional music]* But the angel said, "Fear not, for I bring you good news of great joy for all people: to you is born this day a Savior, who is Christ the Lord. This will be a sign for you: you will find the babe wrapped in cloth and lying in a manger." And suddenly there was with the angel a multitude of heavenly host, praising God and saying, "Glory to God, in the highest; peace on earth, good will to men." *[At "and suddenly" Mel gets on the chair or stool and becomes quite dramatic, but not silly. Mom becomes still, mesmerized by the words. After last line, music fades and Mel turns to find Mom dabbing her eyes with a kitchen towel.]*

MEL: What are you crying for, Mom? *[Gets down from chair]* I said it was good news.

MOM: It certainly is, honey. Very good news.

MEL: Do you want me to listen to your part now?

MOM: My part? Oh, I'm not in the program tonight.

MEL: But I heard you practicing your lines over and over today.

MOM: Oh that. *[Pause]* Yes, Mel, I'd love to have you listen to my part. *[Stands tall and faces C; with much feeling]* Jesus is the reason for the season!

MEL: Good job, Mom. Is my costume OK?

MOM: It's perfect, honey, just perfect.

Alterations

The insults exchanged between Kid1 and Kid2 can be almost anything that would lend itself to a "did too"/"did not" or "are too"/"am not" format. Be sensitive to your audience, though, and do your best to avoid anything that might be offensive.

The ending of this sketch could be slightly modified to show all family members grasping the truth of the season and the error of their ways by having Kid1 and Kid2 followed by Dad entering UR as Mel steps up on the kitchen stool during her final monologue. As Mel finishes, Dad crosses to Mom and puts an arm around her, and Kid1 and Kid2 "make up" with an exchange of playful slugs to the arm or some other appropriate gesture.

Hints

This sketch is better for senior high or older. Junior high can pull it off, but parts need to be selected carefully. Younger students sometimes have a harder time portraying ages other than their own. Of course, the ideal situation would be a mixed cast with players actually the same age as their characters. Again, exceptional children would have to be found to have a polished performance.

If Mel's ending dialogue is too difficult for a player to memorize, allow the player to read it off an index card, just as children sometimes do in Christmas programs.

Put an extra tray of cookies in the oven just in case Mom doesn't get a "next batch" in. That way when she goes to retrieve another burning batch, she won't be horrified to find the oven empty!

Discussion Questions

1. In what ways do your actions during the holidays communicate Christmas is about something other than Jesus?

2. What can you do to make sure your words and your actions proclaim that "Jesus is the reason for the season"?

3. Choose one thing you will do this holiday season to live out the real reason we celebrate.

A Father's Love

THEME: No matter what God's children do, they cannot be separated from their heavenly Father's love.

SETTING: Father's house just after breakfast. Also, on another part of the stage clearly separated from Father's house, a city alley.

CHARACTERS: Narrator (Narr), Father, Angelina (age 5–6), Kevin (age 9–10), Charity (age 7–8), Calvin (age 15–16), Unnamed child (any age), and José (age 12–13). Ideally, the children should be of various ethnic backgrounds.

COSTUMES: Everyday street clothes may be worn by all characters except Father, who should be wearing a suit and tie. Jose's clothes should look worn and dirty.

PROPS: Small kitchen table set for breakfast, a couple of chairs, briefcase, trash can, boxes, old newspapers, glass bottles (all optional).

[Father should be C and the children form a line from C to L.]

[☞ 8–Background music]

NARR: Once there was a father who had many children. He loved each one dearly. Every morning, before he left for work, the children would all line up to hug him good-bye. As he took his sons and daughters into his arms, he would speak to each one tenderly.

[Angelina jumps into Father's arms. He hugs her as he speaks.]

(From Laura L. Martinez, *Drama for the Dramatically Challenged: Church Plays Made Easy* © 2000 by Judson Press. Reproduced by permission.)

FATHER: Oh, my little Angelina, you are truly my sweet little angel. *[Kevin steps up as Father puts Angelina down]* Kevin, how I love you, my son. *[Father hugs him. Kevin steps aside and Charity moves toward Father who kneels down and puts his arms around her.]* Charity, you're such a precious girl. I will think of you today. *[Calvin steps toward Father and extends his hand playfully. Father shakes it firmly and then pulls the boy to himself in a big hug. Calvin embraces Father just as wholeheartedly.]* Calvin, you are growing into such a fine young man. I am proud of you. *[Father hugs Unnamed child as Narr continues]*

NARR: But one day, as the father hugged the last waiting child, he was overcome with panic.

FATHER: *[Looks around frantically]* José—where is José?

NARR: The other children looked down nervously.

FATHER: What is it? Where is my José? Calvin, tell me, if you know.

CALVIN: Not here, Father,

NARR: Calvin replied.

CALVIN: He said he didn't want to stand in line like a little child to hug his father. He went outside before breakfast.

NARR: The father was instantly distraught. He raced out the door calling for his beloved child.

[Father should use the audience area for his search, going up and down the aisles. As he does, all the children exit L. José should appear very discreetly and huddle at stage R in the "alley."]

FATHER: José! . . . José!

NARR: He went from house to house looking for his son. He searched parks and empty lots. Hour after weary hour, he looked for the boy. He asked neighbors and friends, even strangers if they had seen him. Most had not. Some thought perhaps he had gone this way or that, but they couldn't be sure. Finally, after days of relentlessly seeking his lost son, the father found him. José was dirty and cold, huddled in an alley full of garbage and broken glass.

FATHER: My son!

NARR: exclaimed the father.

FATHER: José, my child, I have found you! Come, let me take you home.

NARR: He reached for the boy's hand, but the boy did not reach back. The father was dismayed.

FATHER: What's the matter, son? Don't you want to come home?

JOSÉ: I can't,

NARR: the son replied flatly.

FATHER: Of course you can,

NARR: said the father.

FATHER: Take my hand.

JOSÉ: No,

NARR: said the son.

JOSÉ: You don't understand. You don't know where I've been. You don't know what I've done.

FATHER: José, my child, I love you. You belong with me. I have searched for you for days without rest. *[Pause]* Give me your hand. It is time to go home.

NARR: The son began to reach up weakly.

JOSÉ: I don't think I can walk.

FATHER: Then I will carry you,

NARR: said the father, and he reached down and scooped the boy into his arms. And as he did, he hugged him and spoke tenderly.

FATHER: José, my precious son. How I have longed for you, my child.

[If the Father is physically able, he should carry the boy offstage—down the aisle and out the back of the auditorium or sanctuary if possible.]

Alterations

If your actor playing Father cannot carry José, simply have them freeze in their embrace for three seconds after the last line and then exit the stage (see "The End" on page 11).

Narr may be seated on a stool stage R or off stage altogether, unseen by the audience. If you choose to have Narr in the audience's sight, he or she should be familiar enough with the piece to be able to look away from the script and make eye contact with the audience. Having Narr memorize the story is also an option, but only if it is memorized well. Struggling for dialogue or mixing up lines will cause confusion and destroy the mood of the piece.

This piece began as a short story and could be performed effectively with Narr reading the entire skit, including spoken lines, and having the players simply act out the physical movements. The accompanying CD includes tracks that provide for additional options: a live reading with only background music, a voice-over for Narr with background music (℗ **9**), or a pantomime to an entirely prerecorded dialogue with music (℗ **10**). In the pantomime option, the actors should stay in character, showing appropriate emotion with body language, gestures, and posture. They should *not* mouth the words, with the possible exception of the father mouthing José's name as he calls for him. (Try the latter in rehearsal. If it looks the least bit odd or exaggerated, don't do it.) When performing the piece this way, it is important for Narr to read at a pace that allows all appropriate action to take place. Again, Narr may be seen or unseen.

Hints

You should cast actual young people in the parts of the children. Do *not* have adults play these roles. You can deviate a bit from the recommended ages if necessary. If you use young children, you may find it helpful to add a Mother to your cast. She can help line up the young children after they have their turn at hugging Father and assist in getting the children offstage at the appropriate time in an orderly fashion. This will look more natural to the audience than seeing the younger children looking toward the director for cues.

Depending on the size of your auditorium, you may choose not to have Father visibly search for the child throughout the narration. If your area is small, have Father disappear offstage for a bit, so he is not having to retrace his steps to fill time during the narration.

You may wish to have Father actually ask audience members, "Have you seen my son?" However, this should be done quietly so as not to distract from the narration. Also, the actor playing the part must be able to stay in character while doing this. If you are afraid he will have trouble doing so, do not have him talk to audience members, as it could have a humorous effect.

Father should take any opportunity to make his appearance more and more disheveled as he searches. He might take off his jacket, carry it for a bit, and then leave it behind. He may loosen his tie as well. If your player exits the auditorium or is temporarily out of the audience's view (e.g., in the very back of the auditorium and so behind the audience), he should untuck his shirt and possibly mess up his hair a bit by running his fingers through it–being careful not to get carried away and make his appearance comical.

Father must be careful to speak loudly enough for the audience to hear him. Explain to the children in the skit that, although it may sound like Father is speaking too loudly, he needs to do so in order for everyone in the audience to hear him. Also, be careful to position Father so he is able to be seen and heard when talking with José. (See "Actors' Positions" on page 3 and also "Being Heard" on page 8.) Using a lapel microphone is not recommended, since it will make a lot of noise each time Father embraces one of the children.

Should you choose to use props and furniture, be sure to place them in such a way so as not to detract from or block any action, especially the interaction at the end between Father and José.

You need not adhere to the stage directions provided in the script. It may work better for you to place José at stage L where the other children line up. Their exit and Father's activity in the audience may work as good cover for getting José on stage without much notice from the audience. Try not to draw attention to José until Father sees him. José should remain completely still until he is found by Father.

Because this sketch is obviously an allegory of God the Father's love for *all* of his children, the ideal cast should include various ethnic backgrounds. If, however, this is not possible, you may wish to change the names of some of the children to be more representative of your cast's ethnic make-up.

Discussion Questions

1. What is your first reaction to this story?

2. Can you relate to José? Have you ever experienced God's love and grace in a similar way? Have you ever run away from God's love?

3. Read Matthew 18:2–4. Why do some people struggle with the concept of being a *child* of God?

4. Look again at the theme of this skit. Do you agree with this concept? (Check out Romans 8:35,38–39.)

Guest Speaker: Jesus

THEME: Following Jesus is difficult and costly; some may not be willing to make the necessary sacrifices.

SETTING: Wherever this skit is performed. For example, if this is performed at a youth rally, then the setting is a youth rally, where the "speaker" takes the stage to give the devotional message.

CHARACTERS: Jesus, five to twelve congregation members (both male and female; only five with speaking parts: C1, C2, C3, C4, C5).

COSTUMES: Jesus could be dressed in historical costume, preferably a white robe with a colored shoulder drape and sandals, or in street clothes appropriate for the setting. (Our Jesus forgot his historical costume, and we found the sketch was still very powerful.) Actors playing congregation members should be dressed as typical for the occasion (for example, worship service, youth rally, etc.).

PROPS: A podium and microphone (optional).

[Those playing congregation members are already seated in the audience. Without introduction, Jesus steps onto platform, behind podium and microphone if applicable, and begins speaking.]

JESUS: *[With the feeling of speaking good news]* If any want to become my followers, let them deny themselves and take up their cross and follow me. For those who want to save their life will lose

---

it, and those who lose their life for my sake will find it. For what will it profit them if they gain the whole world but forfeit their life?

C1: Uh, excuse me, Jesus? *[Rising and moving toward the front]* I'm sorry, but I just feel like I have to say something here. I think maybe you should reconsider your presentation a little and possibly tone down the self-denial stuff—just a bit. It's gonna turn people off. It's a different world now, Jesus. A person has to look out for himself, do what's in his own best interest, ya know? There's nothing wrong with that. Certainly I can take care of my own needs and desires and still serve you.

JESUS: No one can serve two masters; for a slave will either hate the one and love the other, or be devoted to the one and despise the other. You have been crucified with me; and it is no longer you who live, but I who live in you.

C1: Well, you certainly won't win many followers that way! *[Exits down center aisle]*

JESUS: Whoever does not carry the cross and follow me cannot be my disciple. For which of you, intending to build a tower, does not first sit down and estimate the cost, to see whether he has enough to complete it? Otherwise, when he has laid a foundation and is not able to finish, all who see it will begin to ridicule him, saying, "This fellow began to build and was not able to finish."

C2: *[Standing]* Hey, whoa. I thought salvation was free. *[Moving to the front]* What's all this cost talk? I'm all for accepting you as Savior, Jesus, but then I've got a life to live.

JESUS: I appeal to you, by the mercies of God, to present your bodies as a living sacrifice, holy and acceptable to God, which is your spiritual worship.

C2: I thought *you* were the sacrifice! *[Exits down center aisle]*

C3: *[Rising]* Yeah, and what do you mean by "holy"?

JESUS: As he who called you is holy, be holy yourselves in all your conduct; for it is written, "You shall be holy, for I am holy."

C3: *[Going to the front]* What you're asking is impossible. I mean, come on, look at the world we live in—temptations are everywhere. You can't possibly expect us to be . . . *[Pauses as if looking for the right word]*

JESUS: Perfect?

C3: Well, yeah. Besides, it's not like we live under the Old Testament law. I believe it's *your* Word that says we are not under the law, but under grace.

JESUS: Do you not know that if you present yourselves to anyone as obedient slaves, you are slaves of the one whom you obey, either of sin, which leads to death, or of obedience, which leads to righteousness?

C3: Hey, I'm not *anyone's* slave. *[Exits]*

JESUS: *[Shakes head, looks out over congregation]* Very truly, I tell you, I am the gate for the sheep. All who came before me are thieves and bandits; but the sheep did not listen to them. I am the gate. Whoever enters by me will be saved, and will come in and go out and find pasture. The thief comes only to steal and kill and destroy. I came that they may have life, and have it abundantly. I am the way, and the truth, and the life. No one comes to the Father except through me.

C4: *[Standing]* That sounds like you're saying you're the only way to heaven. *[Approaching front]* Jesus, people today need options. I mean, there are lots of good philosophies and religions out there. Who are we to say Christianity has a corner on the truth? So what if one person prays to Buddha or Muhammad and another calls on a "Higher Power." Those are all just names for God, right? So ultimately we're all praying to the same Person. Your way is so narrow-minded!

JESUS: The gate *is* narrow and the road is hard that leads to life, and there are few who find it. Enter through the narrow gate; for the gate is wide and the road is easy that leads to destruction, and there are many who take it.

[C4 exits down center aisle. C5, along with several others, rise from audience and approach the front.]

JESUS: *[To this group]* Do you also wish to go away?

C5: Lord, to whom can we go? You have the truth. To turn away from you and chase after a lie would be utter foolishness. You have the words of eternal life.

[Jesus descends from platform to meet them]

JESUS: *[Very serious]* You understand, this will cost you everything.

C5: We know.

JESUS: Then come, *[Smiles]* follow me.

[Jesus leads followers offstage—preferably in a direction different from the one taken by those who previously exited: for example, a side door at stage L]

NOTE: Scripture references in order of appearance, all taken from the New Revised Standard Version: Matthew 16:24–26; Matthew 6:24; Galatians 2:19–20; Luke 14:27–30; Romans 12:1; 1 Peter 1:15–16; Romans 6:16; John 10:7–10; John 14:6; Matthew 7:14; 7:13; John 6:67–68.

Alteration

If you do not have additional cast members to go to the front with C5, change his response to "Lord, to whom can *I* go? . . ."

Hints

The person playing Jesus does not need to have a beard and long hair. If the actor is skilled in the part, the audience will overlook even a Jesus with an unusual hairstyle or color (see "Does Jesus Need a Beard?" on page 17).

Scatter your extra players throughout the audience. As players with speaking parts exit, have one or two extras exit too. When the last goes forward to meet Jesus, have one or two extras go along. If you do not have many extras, have them go with the last two or three players only. For instance, if you only have three extras, have one go out with C3 and the other two exit with C5. Players exiting together should not talk to one another or walk side by side. They should leave with a look of disgust, disappointment, disbelief, etc. and avoid making eye contact with other members of the audience.

Make sure all players choose aisle seats so they do not have to squeeze past other audience members. Also make sure that those with speaking parts are close enough to the front that they are able to walk all the way to the podium area as they speak their lines. It might be a good idea to reserve their seats with signs.

If possible, have the name of this sketch printed in your bulletin or program, but without quotation marks or any reference to it as the drama portion of the program. Do not have anyone introduce the piece; simply begin at the appropriate time in the service.

Be aware of the need for extra vocal projection from the cast members in the audience (unless you have the resources to put a wireless lapel microphone on each of them). They will be speaking with their backs to the audience as they approach the front, and it is important for the audience to hear these lines clearly. When the actors reach the front, have them cheat out so their bodies are turned out slightly toward the audience. Their lines, however, should be addressed to Jesus and out over the audience, not directly to the audience. (See "Actors' positions" on pages 3–4 for an explanation of "cheating out.")

Discussion Questions

1. What is it about these hard sayings of Jesus that keep would-be followers away?

2. Do you think Jesus went a bit overboard with some of his demands? Why or why not?

3. Do you think many Christians take these passages seriously? What evidence do you see for your answer?

4. In John 6:68, what reason does Peter give for not abandoning Jesus and his hard teachings? What does that mean?

His Love Endures Forever
THREE READINGS

Psalm 136 was most likely intended to be read with a chorus of people proclaiming "His love endures forever" after each phrase that extols God's goodness and power. In the following three readings, you have a wonderful opportunity to take what many modern Christians find to be rather unnecessary repetition and to help it accomplish what it was intended to do–wake us up to God's unfailing love!

A READING OF PSALM 136 (NIV)

THEME: God's love is eternal.

CHARACTERS: Reader, Chorus (8 to 10 individuals who read in unison).

PROPS: Black folder containing script for Reader.

[Reader stands C; Chorus stands in a row UC.]

READER: *[With enthusiasm and feeling]* Give thanks to the LORD, for he is good.

CHORUS: His love endures forever.

READER: Give thanks to the God of the gods.

CHORUS: His love endures forever.

READER: Give thanks to the Lord of lords:

CHORUS: His love endures forever.

READER: to him who alone does great wonders,

CHORUS: His love endures forever.

READER: who by his understanding made the heavens,

CHORUS: His love endures forever.

READER: who spread out the earth upon the waters,

CHORUS: His love endures forever.

READER: who made the great lights—

CHORUS: His love endures forever.

READER: the sun to govern the day,

CHORUS: His love endures forever.

READER: the moon and the stars to govern the night;

CHORUS: His love endures forever.

READER: to him who struck down the firstborn of Egypt

CHORUS: His love endures forever.

READER: and brought Israel out from among them

CHORUS: His love endures forever.

READER: with a mighty hand and outstretched arm,

CHORUS: His love endures forever.

READER: to him who divided the Red Sea asunder

CHORUS: His love endures forever.

READER: and brought Israel through the midst of it,

CHORUS: His love endures forever.

READER: but swept Pharaoh and his army into the Red Sea,

CHORUS: His love endures forever.

READER: to him who led his people through the desert,

CHORUS: His love endures forever.

READER: who struck down great kings,

CHORUS: His love endures forever.

READER: and killed mighty kings—

CHORUS: His love endures forever.

READER: and gave their land as an inheritance,

CHORUS: His love endures forever.

READER: an inheritance to his servant Israel;

CHORUS: His love endures forever.

READER: to the one who remembered us in our low estate

CHORUS: His love endures forever.

READER: and freed us from our enemies,

CHORUS: His love endures forever.

READER: and who gives food to every creature.

CHORUS: His love endures forever.

READER: Give thanks to the God of heaven.

CHORUS: His love endures forever.

NOTE: Verses 19 and 20 have been omitted. Since most audiences will be unfamiliar with the names mentioned in these verses, their inclusion may be distracting. If you feel strongly about including them, however, please feel free to do so.

A READING FROM EPHESIANS 1:3-14 (NRSV) WITH THE REFRAIN OF PSALM 136 (NIV)

THEME: God's love is eternal, as described in Ephesians 1:3–14.

CHARACTERS: Reader, Chorus (8 to10 individuals who read in unison).

PROPS: Black folder containing script for Reader.

[Reader stands C; Chorus stands in a row UC.]

READER: *[With enthusiasm]* Blessed be the God and Father of our Lord Jesus Christ,

CHORUS: His love endures forever.

READER: who has blessed us in Christ with every spiritual blessing in the heavenly places,

CHORUS: His love endures forever.

READER: just as he chose us in Christ before the foundation of the world to be holy and blameless before him in love.

CHORUS: His love endures forever.

READER: He destined us for adoption as his children through Jesus Christ, according to the good pleasure of his will,

CHORUS: His love endures forever.

READER: to the praise of his glorious grace that he freely bestowed on us in the Beloved.

CHORUS: His love endures forever.

READER: In Him we have redemption through his blood,

CHORUS: His love endures forever.

READER: the forgiveness of our trespasses,

CHORUS: His love endures forever.

READER: according to the riches of his grace that he lavished on us.

CHORUS: His love endures forever.

READER: with all wisdom and insight he has made known to us the mystery of his will,

CHORUS: His love endures forever.

READER: according to his good pleasure that he set forth in Christ,

CHORUS: His love endures forever.

READER: as a plan for the fullness of time, to gather up all things in him,

CHORUS: His love endures forever.

READER: things in heaven and things on earth.

CHORUS: His love endures forever.

READER: In Christ we have also obtained an inheritance,

CHORUS: His love endures forever.

READER: having been destined according to the purpose of him who accomplishes all things according to his counsel and will,

CHORUS: His love endures forever.

READER: so that we, who were the first to set our hope on Christ, might live for the praise of his glory.

CHORUS: His love endures forever.

READER: In him you also, when you had heard the word of truth, the gospel of your salvation, and had believed in him, were marked with the seal of the promised Holy Spirit;

CHORUS: His love endures forever.

READER: this is the pledge of our inheritance toward redemption as God's own people,

CHORUS: His love endures forever.

READER: to the praise of his glory.

CHORUS: His love endures forever.

NOTE: The refrain of this reading is taken from Psalm 136 from the New International Version; the Reader's lines are taken from Ephesians 1:3–14 from the New Revised Standard Version. You may prefer to use the New Revised Standard Version of the chorus, which is "His steadfast love endures forever." If you use this reading in conjunction with the previous piece based on Psalm 136, however, you may wish to leave the Chorus's line the same to prevent confusion and mistakes by your group.

A READING FROM SELECTED VERSES OF ROMANS 8 (NRSV) WITH THE REFRAIN OF PSALM 136 (NIV)

THEME: God's eternal love, as described in Romans 8.

CHARACTERS: Reader, Chorus of readers (8 to10 individuals who read in unison).

PROPS: Black folder containing script for Reader.

[Reader stands C; Chorus stands in a row UC.]

READER: *[With enthusiasm]* If God is for us, who is against us?

CHORUS: His love endures forever.

READER: He who did not withhold his own Son, but gave him up for all of us, will he not with him also give us everything else?

CHORUS: His love endures forever.

READER: Who will bring any charge against God's elect?

CHORUS: His love endures forever.

READER: It is God who justifies. Who is to condemn?

CHORUS: His love endures forever.

READER: It is Christ Jesus, who died, yes, who was raised, who is at the right hand of God, who indeed intercedes for us.

CHORUS: His love endures forever.

READER: Who will separate us from the love of Christ?

CHORUS: His love endures forever.

READER: Will hardship, or distress, or persecution,

CHORUS: His love endures forever.

READER: or famine, or nakedness, or peril, or sword?

CHORUS: His love endures forever.

READER: No, in all these things we are more than conquerors through him who loved us.

CHORUS: His love endures forever.

READER: For I am convinced that neither death, nor life, nor angels, nor rulers, nor things present, nor things to come,

CHORUS: His love endures forever.

READER: nor powers, nor height, nor depth, nor anything else in all creation, will be able to separate us from the love of God in Christ Jesus our Lord.

CHORUS: His love endures forever.

READER: There is therefore now no condemnation for those who are in Christ Jesus.

CHORUS: His love endures forever.

READER: For all who are led by the Spirit of God are children of God.

CHORUS: His love endures forever.

READER: For you did not receive a spirit of slavery to fall back into fear, but you have received a spirit of adoption.

CHORUS: His love endures forever.

READER: When we cry "Abba! Father!" it is that very Spirit bearing witness with our spirit that we are children of God,

CHORUS: His love endures forever.

READER: and if children, then heirs, heirs of God and joint heirs with Christ.

CHORUS: His love endures forever.

NOTE: The refrain of this reading is taken from Psalm 136 in the New International Version; the Reader's lines, in the order in which they appear, are taken from the New Revised Standard Version of the eighth chapter of Romans, verses 31b–35, verses 37–39, verse 1, and verses 14–17a. You may prefer to use the New Revised Standard Version reading for the Chorus's refrain as well, which is "His steadfast love endures forever." If you use this reading in conjunction with either of the previous readings, however, you may wish to leave the words of the refrain the same to prevent confusion and mistakes by your group.

Alterations

These pieces may be used in the same service or performed as independent pieces. If you choose the former option, I strongly recommend using the Psalm 136 reading and only one of the New Testament readings rather than squeezing all three into the same program. If you choose this option, you may have the same person act as Reader in both pieces or choose different Readers. Avoid reading the pieces in succession; space them out with music or other program features. Placing as many as two to three other elements between the readings would be advisable.

If you do not have enough people for a large Chorus, find at least four people and turn the piece into a readers' theater without movement (see "Readers' Theater" on page 12). Assign the lines of the Chorus to the four members in various combinations. Here's an example of how I would distribute the initial lines of the first piece:

> **READER:** Give thanks to the Lord, for he is good.
>
> **ALL:** His love endures forever.
>
> **READER:** Give thanks to the God of the gods.
>
> **1:** His love endures forever.
>
> **READER:** Give thanks to the Lord of lords:
>
> **2:** His love endures forever.
>
> **READER:** to him who alone does great wonders.
>
> **1 & 4:** His love endures forever.

In this scenario, the Chorus readers should also have black folders with scripts that highlight the parts they are to read.

If you have the ability to assemble a large Chorus (twelve or more people), you may want to position them in groups of three or four throughout the room. The more people you have, the more creative you can be. Use the balcony, the front, the back, the side aisles, the choir loft. These groups could all read in unison, or you could distribute the lines to various sections, similar to the readers' theater example above. Again, it would be a good idea to give Chorus members black folders with scripts. You may also wish to have a lead reader in each group to help ensure unity.

Hints

At first, the Chorus's role may seem like a "no brainer," but it may actually take quite a bit of rehearsal. It is very important that the members of the Chorus read together and that they don't allow their recurring line to fall flat. There is not, however, a lot of room for "creative interpretation" since all members must speak in strict unison. Work with the Chorus to help the members deliver their line with joy without getting carried away and detracting from the Reader's lines. It may be wise to have a leader among the Chorus who is responsible for setting the pace and starting each line. This is not to say that everyone waits to hear the leader's voice before starting and so misses the first word each time. What having a leader *does* ensure is that the line always starts without hesitation. If you position your Chorus in a half circle, members may be able to see the leader in their peripheral vision and the visual contact should help keep everyone together. I cannot stress enough the need to rehearse the Chorus role thoroughly. It may look easy, but the performance must be absolutely polished to give the full effect.

It would be wise to have your Reader spend some time reading the original scripture passages before practicing the piece as written above. This will help him or her get a feel for the meaning of the main verses and so convey that meaning more effectively when the verses are broken up by the Chorus. The Reader may memorize his or her lines, but if this option is chosen, the memorization must be down cold! Hesitation during the performance will break the rhythm of the piece. Also, the Reader's lines should be delivered with appropriate emotion and excitement. Be careful not to let your Reader get melodramatic, however.

Discussion Questions for the Reading from Psalm 136

1. Whenever we find repetition in Scripture, it is there for a reason. What do you think the purpose is here?

2. Read Proverbs 19:22 and 20:6 from the New International Version. How does Psalm 136 answer this desire?

3. Read Lamentations 3:22–23. Share what it means to you that God's love and mercy toward you are unfailing?

For the Reading from Ephesians 1

4. Which parts of this reading from Ephesians stand out to you as evidence of God's enduring love for you?

5. What purposes for the life of every believer do you see in these verses? (There are at least three.)

6. What does it mean that God has lavished his grace on us?

7. Look at Ephesians 1:13–14. What "insurance" do you have that God's love for you will endure forever?

For the Reading from Romans 8

8. Which parts of this reading from Romans stand out to you as evidence of God's enduring love for you?

9. What obstacles in life seem to separate you from God's love? How do these verses reassure you in the face of such obstacles?

10. What does it mean to you to be adopted by God? How does it reaffirm the concept of God's everlasting love for you?

I Was Thinking

THEME: God chose to create us knowing that he would have to make the ultimate sacrifice to save us.

CHARACTERS: Reader, male or female.

PROPS: Podium or script folder; candles with drip guards placed in all inside aisle seats; candle for reader; candle and lighter for helper in the back of the auditorium (see "Hints" below).

READER: I was thinking . . . *[Pause]* I was thinking how we tend to see the story of the first Christmas as a complete story in and of itself. Mary. Joseph. Baby on the way. Long journey to Bethlehem. No room in the inn. A stable. Baby Jesus is born. Angels appear to shepherds. They find the babe and his mother and spread the Good News. The end.

But that's really just a chapter in a much larger drama. It starts before the Promised Land, before Moses and the burning bush, before Abraham and Sarah, before Adam and Eve. It starts even before the beginning when God spoke the first words of creation—"Let there be light."

For before there was anything, there was God—God the Father, God the Son, God the Holy Spirit. The baffling mystery of the triune God—three in one—long before there was anyone to ponder the mystery. God was, as God is: all-knowing and all-present—transcending time and space. So before God spoke the words that would set creation into motion, God knew. He knew that after the light and the perfection, there would be darkness and sin. There would be murder and drunkenness, slander and idolatry. And God knew exactly what it would cost him. And God said the words anyway, "Let there be light." But before the words were spoken, 1 Peter 1:20 tells us, God made a plan: Christ "was chosen before the creation of the world" (NIV).

God knew what would happen. God could have stopped the creation before it was started. So why didn't he? Was God lonely? No, that would imply God lacked something. I think that maybe, just maybe, the thought of you, of us, was so wonderful God decided he'd rather suffer and die than to be without us, just the thought of you was that precious to God. God could have said, "Never mind." But instead God said, "Let there be light." [♪ 11–*optional music*] [*Start candle lighting from the back of the sanctuary to the front*] And there was light. And it was good. And there was sin and darkness and separation from God. And there was Mary and Joseph and a long journey to Bethlehem. There was no room in the inn, but there was room in the stable. Baby Jesus was born and he grew up and he lived and he died and he rose again that we might have the light of his salvation.

But even that's not the end of the story. For Jesus has promised to return and call all his children home to be with him forever and ever. A story without an end. May he find us on that day serving him and sharing his light.

Hints

This piece should be read slowly enough to allow the audience to contemplate the words. The reader should be well rehearsed to ensure a smooth read with appropriate inflection and emotion.

The reader or another individual should explain the candle lighting before the reading begins by saying something like the following: "Those of you sitting on the inside aisle will find a small candle in your seat. During this morning's reading we will be passing a flame from the back of the sanctuary to the front. Someone in the back will tap you on the shoulder at a certain point in the reading. Turn around, light your candle from theirs, and then tap the person in front of you. When the flame reaches the front and the reading is done, I will come down and light my candle with the help of the two people in the front row."

Have one or two people in the back of the sanctuary following along with the script and being prepared to light a candle and begin the lighting process at the appropriate time. The timing of the candle lighting may need to be adjusted based on the distance from the back of the room to the front. If the timing is a bit off and the reading is done before the flame is passed all the way to the front, the reader should step forward to the front row of seats and wait in silence. This continues the contemplative mood and allows the audience more time to ponder what they have heard.

If you are using this reading as part of a Christmas service, you may want to have candles for all congregation members. After the people sitting near the aisle pass the flame forward, they should then pass it to the person sitting next to them and so begin lighting their row's candles as well.

I used this piece as an Advent reading and used my candle to light the candles on the Advent wreath. It could also be used to lead into a time of prayer.

Discussion Questions

1. Have you ever thought about God knowing "what he was getting into" when he chose to create us?

2. Read 1 Peter 1:18–20. How do you feel about God's "informed decision"?

3. What should our response be?

The Jill Donapew Show

THEME: There is plenty of evidence for the resurrection of Jesus, both biblically and logically.

SETTING: Talk show

CHARACTERS: Jill Donapew, Announcer, John, Mary Magdalene, Roman Guard, Scribe, Ima Pain, Caller, Pharisee, two members of audience (Audience1, Audience2).

COSTUMES: Jill and Ima should be dressed in business suits. John, Mary, and the Roman Guard can be dressed in historical costumes or modern street clothes. The Pharisee should be in a crazy disguise, which could include a wig and a pair of glasses with a plastic nose or a Lone Ranger mask. (We put our guy in a dress!)

PROPS: Microphone (preferably handheld) for Jill, headset if Announcer will be seen, huge Bible or other very large book that would pass for a Bible for the Scribe to read out of, briefcase for Ima, six chairs, applause signs, note cards for Jill.

*[♅ **12**–music and applause]*

[Applause signs are held up as theme music plays and Jill comes down the aisle toward the stage, where guests are seated in chairs]

ANNOUNCER: Here's your host–Jill Donapew!

[Jill picks up a mike lying on the floor of the stage. Theme music fades as Jill begins speaking.]

(From Laura L. Martinez, *Drama for the Dramatically Challenged: Church Plays Made Easy* © 2000 by Judson Press. Reproduced by permission.)

JILL: Thank you. Let me introduce our guests for today's show *[glancing at note cards]:* John, one of Jesus' twelve disciples who actually saw the empty tomb of Jesus; Mary, also a follower of Jesus–she claims to have been the first to see Jesus after he was resurrected; a member of the imperial Roman guard who was present at the death of Jesus and stood guard at the tomb Saturday night to Sunday morning, during which time the body disappeared; a scribe of the law who will be sharing with us Old Testament prophecies about the Messiah; Miss Ima Pain, a lawyer for the CLUA who is bringing a lawsuit against all Christians and against God himself–we'll tell you why; and finally a guest who has agreed to appear only if his identity is kept secret–we can tell you he is a pharisee who says he was involved in a cover-up scheme the day Jesus' body was reported missing. We'd like to thank all our guests for appearing on today's show.

[Applause signs are held up]

[🎧 13–applause]

JILL: John, let's start with you. It's been several years now since Jesus' supposed resurrection. Has your story changed at all?

JOHN: No way. Now that I look back, I realize Jesus had been telling us all along that he would suffer and die and then be raised on the third day. For some reason it just never made any sense until it actually happened. When I saw the grave clothes lying there, but no body, then I believed! But I have to admit, when Mary and the girls first came to us and told us about the empty tomb and having seen angels, well . . . we thought they'd been carrying those burial spices and herbs a little too close to their noses, if you know what I mean.

JILL: Whoa, whoa, angels? Come on, Mary. Just what kind of herbs *were* you ladies carrying?

MARY: I don't like what you're implying, Jill.

JILL: I'm sorry, Mare. I'm just playing the devil's advocate here.

[Mary and John gasp and make crosses with their fingers in Jill's direction]

JILL: It's just a figure of speech.

MARY: Perhaps you should refigure your speech.

JILL: Yes, ma'am.

MARY: Yes, there were angels—two to be exact. When we arrived at the tomb, the huge stone covering the entrance had been rolled away. I ran back to the disciples and told them someone had taken Jesus' body. The other women stayed behind and looked inside the tomb. Two angels told them Jesus was alive. He had risen just like he said he would.

JILL: Isn't it also true, Mary, that you claim to have actually *seen* Jesus alive that same morning?

MARY: Yes. I followed John and Peter back to the tomb. After they left, I knelt down in front of the tomb weeping. I heard a voice behind me asking why I was crying. Through my tears I didn't recognize the person. I assumed it was the gardener. But then he said my name. I knew in an instant it was Jesus!

SCRIBE: That's blasphemy! If he was resurrected, then you are saying this Jesus was the Messiah.

JOHN: Exactly.

SCRIBE: Unkosher hogwash!

JILL: *[Checking note cards]* OK, let me say that you are a scribe, a scholar of the Scriptures, and that you have come here today to share with us some of the prophecies regarding the Messiah which you claim will show Jesus could not have been that Messiah. Give us an example.

SCRIBE: Gladly. Psalm 22:18 says, "They divide my clothes among themselves, and for my clothing they cast lots." And Psalm 34:20 says of the Righteous One that God "keeps all their bones; not one of them will be broken." This can't be true of Jesus since he was crucified just before the sabbath. It is the custom to break the legs of the crucified and take the body down before sunset, even if the person isn't dead yet.

GUARD: Jill, I think I'd be the one to address this one. As a member of the Roman guard, I was present at the crucifixion of Jesus, and those prophecies were fulfilled. The soldiers did divide Jesus' clothes among them, and they gambled for his tunic. As far as broken bones, I'm no doctor, but I do know we did not break his legs before taking him down. There was no need since he was already dead and couldn't possibly have crawled away.

JILL: You're sure?

GUARD: I pierced his side with my spear. Blood and water came out. He was dead all right.

SCRIBE: OK, fine. But what about Micah 5:2? "You, O Bethlehem . . . from you shall come forth for me one who is to rule in Israel, whose origin is from of old." The Messiah is to be born in Bethlehem.

JOHN: Jesus was.

SCRIBE: Yeah? Well . . . Isaiah 7:14: "Look, the virgin is with child and shall bear a son." So there!

MARY: Mary, the mother of Jesus, is a close personal friend of mine. We've talked many times about the miraculous events surrounding Jesus' birth. And without getting too personal right here on national television, I can say without a doubt that Mary was definitely a virgin at the time of Jesus' birth.

JILL: Uh-huh, well, we have a caller on the line with a question. Go ahead, caller.

[🎧 14–optional Caller voice-over]

CALLER: Yeah, uh, hi Jill. I'm not sure who to direct this question to, but I've heard some people saying that the Roman guards fell asleep at the tomb and the disciples snuck in and stole the body.

GUARD: Impossible! We never sleep on the job.

JILL: I suppose your job wouldn't last long if you did.

GUARD: Job nothing. Our lives wouldn't last long. The penalty for sleeping on the job is death!

JILL: Perhaps our guest on the end could shed a little light on our caller's question.

PHARISEE: I was one of the Pharisees the guards came to that morning. We were in a panic. The guards were babbling about bright lights and being frozen with fear. Something incredible had happened, though no one was sure what. The bottom line was the body was gone!

JILL: Why didn't you just go public with the news?

PHARISEE: Are you kidding?! We knew those crazy disciples would start making up stories about a resurrection. Jesus had talked about it. We were afraid they'd seize the opportunity to lead others astray.

JILL: So what did you do?

PHARISEE: We made up a story. Paid off the guards to say they'd fallen asleep. We covered for them with their superiors. *[Breaking down]* But it was a lie, Jill. They weren't asleep. I don't know what happened. The story was all a lie.

JILL: *[Going to audience member whose hand is up]* Let's take a question from the audience.

AUDIENCE1: My question is for John. Isn't it true that you and the disciples ambushed the guards and then stole the body?

GUARD: Listen, I don't know what the deal is here, but I didn't come on this show for Bash the Roman Guard Day! What do you think we are, a bunch of sissies? We are highly trained, physically fit fighting machines. A group of ragtag–*[Looks to John]* no offense–fishermen and tax collectors wouldn't stand a chance against us–ambush or otherwise.

JOHN: And even if that did happen, how do you explain all the people who saw Jesus after the resurrection?

PHARISEE: Disciple in a clever disguise?

JILL: OK, well before we run out of time, we need to get to our final guest. *[Refers to note cards]* Ima Pain is a lawyer with the CLUA. She and her colleagues are bringing a suit against the followers of Jesus and against God himself. Ima, tell us what this is all about.

IMA: Well, Jill, Christians claim that the only way to heaven is through Jesus. And I quote, "Jesus said, 'I am the way, and the truth, and the life. No one comes to the Father except through me.'" That is blatant discrimination!

JOHN: Against whom? All people of every ethnic group, every religion, and every socioeconomic class are invited to receive Jesus and so have eternal life.

IMA: Isn't it true that Jesus died for sinners?

JOHN: Yes.

IMA: Ah-ha! So then he discriminates against nonsinners!

MARY: There's no such thing. And I quote, "All have sinned and fall short of the glory of God."

JOHN: "But to all who received him, who believed in his name, he gave power to become children of God."

IMA: Yeah, well, too bad. I'm suing anyway because, because I'm . . . Ima Pain!

[Ima storms off the stage]

JILL: Well, we're out of time. Thank you to all my guests. *[To audience]* We'll see you next time.

[🔊 15–music and applause]

[Jill hurries to an audience member whose hand is up as theme music comes up and applause signs are raised]

AUDIENCE2: A while ago a panel of scholars got together and decided dogs ate the body of Jesus. What about that?

GUARD: Creative.

MARY: But stupid!

[Jill waves to the audience. Applause signs go up again. She heads to the stage and shakes hands with her guests as theme music fades.]

Hints

This would be a great piece in which to include creative commercials. See "Program Additions" on page 10 for some ideas. Also, be sure to look under the heading "Memorizing Lines" on page 9 for some additional helpful hints.

The part of the Pharisee should be played by a rather uninhibited individual who can have fun with the role. Try to cast a male who is not afraid to wear a wig and a dress!

Discussion Questions

1. Why do you think people are so skeptical about the resurrection of Jesus?

2. Are you skeptical?

3. Does a person have to believe in the resurrection of Jesus in order to be a Christian? (See 1 Corinthians 15:12–19.)

4. When it comes to the issue of the resurrection, which character in this sketch do you most identify with and why?

Mary's View of the Cross

THEME: On Good Friday the Messiah, the Deliverer of his people, was killed.

SETTING: Near the cross of Christ as he breathes his last and dies.

CHARACTERS: Mary the mother of Jesus.

COSTUME: Either a period costume or modern dress, preferably dark in color.

[👂 16–rain and thunder with voice-over]

[Mary is on her knees DC. The sound of thunder is heard over the sound system, followed by a man's voice saying, "It is finished." The sound of a storm slowly fades out.]

MARY: *[In disbelief]* No . . . no. *[With more intensity and sorrow]* No . . . noooo!! *[Pause]* Jesus, precious Jesus, my son—God's Son. What have they done to you? What have they done?

They didn't know. They didn't know who you were. They didn't see the angel that announced your coming or feel the baby growing inside without ever having known a man. They didn't know what I knew.

[Reminiscing] Sometimes, when you were a boy, even I would almost forget who you were. You were so much like the other children. And yet, you were different. There was a drive, a determination in you almost from the very beginning and a sense of kindness, a compassion for others, that was always beyond your years.

(From Laura L. Martinez, *Drama for the Dramatically Challenged: Church Plays Made Easy* © 2000 by Judson Press. Reproduced by permission.)

When you grew up and began to teach, so many came to hear. They hung on your every word and some dared to wonder if you were the one promised by the prophets.

And when you came riding into Jerusalem only a few days ago, I thought perhaps—perhaps it was time for you to establish your kingdom. Perhaps finally the naysayers would be silenced. "Hosanna," they cried. "Save us, we pray thee. Hosanna, Son of David."

And then suddenly you went through the temple like a whirlwind. I know you had the right to cleanse your Father's house. But it only added fuel to the fire of your enemies' hatred.

[Sadness growing] And now look what they have done. Look what they have done to their Messiah. The Chosen One promised by God to save his people. And now what hope do we have? What hope could we possibly have? We are of all people most in darkness and doomed. We have killed our Messiah. We have thrown away our only hope. What can we now do? Can God yet save us? Will he?

My son, my precious son, what have we done?

Hints

This piece requires an extremely competent female actor. It should be well rehearsed and polished without neglecting emotion. Much prayerful time should be put into rehearsal. This can be a very powerful, moving piece. I first performed it at a Good Friday observance. Many were touched, but probably none more than myself.

Discussion Questions

1. Read Mark 9:31–32. (See also Luke 24:6–8.) Why do you think Jesus' closest friends had trouble understanding that he would be resurrected?

2. We tend to see the events of Good Friday in light of the resurrection, but what if we didn't know the "end" of the story? Try to imagine being Jesus' mother or Peter, who once confessed, "You are the Christ, the Son of the living God." Assume that Mary and Peter did not grasp the coming of Jesus' resurrection. What sorts of things might have gone through their minds after Jesus died?

3. What do you think might have gone through Mary's mind when she realized Jesus was alive again?

4. Why is it important for us to spend time thinking about the horrible events of Good Friday when we could just skip it and go right to the rejoicing of Easter Sunday?

Nazareth Nightly News

THEME: Theories designed to cause skepticism about the resurrection of Christ can actually cause us to take a closer look at the possibility of the resurrection being real.

SETTING: A TV news studio and on-location sites of the upper room, in front of the temple, on the street below the upper room, and Mary2's living room.

CHARACTERS: Announcer, Susana Joanna, Robby Rabbi, Peter Paul, Annas, Marcus Marcainius, Mary Marry, Mary Magdalene (Mary2).

COSTUMES: Dress clothes for all newspeople (Susana, Robby, Peter, Mary) and Mary2. Marcus should be dressed like a police officer (at least hat and badge, if possible). Annas could be dressed in a black minister's robe or a suit and tie.

PROPS: Large table with chair for Susana, stems only from a cluster of grapes, goblet, plate with cracker crumbs, police "Do Not Cross" tape (optional), small fabric bag with string tied around the top, two chairs or a loveseat and chair, end table with lamp or vase, microphone on a stand for Susana, papers for Robby and Susana to use as notes or news script.

(From Laura L. Martinez, *Drama for the Dramatically Challenged: Church Plays Made Easy* © 2000 by Judson Press. Reproduced by permission.)

[🎧 **17**–*theme music*]

ANNOUNCER: Live from the channel 12 newsroom, it's the Nazareth Nightly News with Susana Joanna and the channel 12 news team.

[Theme music fades as Susana begins speaking]

SUSANA: Good evening, everyone. I'm Susana Joanna. Tonight's top story–the alleged resurrection of Jesus of Nazareth. We've tried to keep you up to date on this bizarre story since word of the empty tomb surfaced just three days after Jesus' crucifixion, but new evidence seems to be uncovered daily. Therefore, we thought it might be good to recap all we've learned so far. We go first to our field reporter Robby Rabbi, who is on scene in the upper room. Robby.

ROBBY: Susana. As you can see, I am standing in a room where a feast took place several days ago. *[Holds up grape stems]* Witnesses say this is the very place where Jesus ate his last meal with his closest friends the night before he was crucified. *[Picks up plate]* This is all that's left of the unleavened bread from this Passover meal. *[Dumps crumbs off plate]* And this, [Picks up cup] this is the very cup Jesus supposedly passed around for all of his disciples to drink from, saying, and I quote, *[Refers to notes]* "This is my blood which is poured out for many." Back to you, Susana.

SUSANA: Robby, that meal would have taken place over two weeks ago. Why hasn't that room been cleaned up yet?

ROBBY: Well, Susana, the authorities sealed off this upper room shortly after Jesus was arrested to be sure nothing would be tampered with in case they needed it for evidence. In fact, we had to climb through a window to get in here.

SUSANA: I see. Thanks, Robby. We go now to Peter Paul, who is outside the temple with one of the chief priests. Peter.

[🎧 **18**–*optional crowd noise*]

PETER: I'm standing in front of the temple in beautiful downtown Jerusalem. This normally majestic scene is marred today by accusations of a conspiracy by the religious leaders to have Jesus killed. With me is Chief Priest Annas. Annas, tell me, how do you respond to such harsh accusations?

ANNAS: They're ridiculous; that's all.

PETER: Some say you paid Judas Iscariot thirty pieces of silver to betray Jesus. What do you say to that?

ANNAS: That's ridiculous.

PETER: Some say he was so upset after doing your dirty work, he tried to return the money. *[In Annas's face]* What do you say to that?!

ANNAS: Ridiculous, this is all ridiculous! You can't prove a thing.

PETER: Oh yeah? My informant—who shall remain nameless—gave me this. *[Holds up a small bag he pulls from a pocket]* This is Judas's money bag. It has his name sewn on the inside. But it's empty! So there, what do you say to that? Huh?

ANNAS: *[Rolls eyes and walks away]* No comment.

PETER: *[Calm and professional again]* Reporting from the Jerusalem temple, I'm Peter Paul. Susana.

SUSANA: Peter. *[To television audience]* We have just received word that reporter Robby Rabbi was apprehended by Roman soldiers as he climbed out one of the windows of the upper room. One of the guards has reportedly told Robby that he was actually present for the crucifixion of Jesus and has agreed to give Robby an exclusive interview before taking him into custody. Robby?

ROBBY: Susana. *[Pause]*

SUSANA: Robby. *[Pause]*

ROBBY: Susana. *[Pause]*

SUSANA: Cut it out!

ROBBY: Sorry, but I've always wanted to do that, *[Looks at soldier who is standing with arms crossed looking very serious]* and this could be my last chance! *[Taking on a more professional demeanor]* With me is Roman Centurion Marcus Marcainius. You say you were present at the crucifixion of Jesus?

MARCUS: That's right.

ROBBY: Some have said Jesus didn't actually die on the cross, that he was still alive when they took him down. How do you respond?

MARCUS: I don't mean to brag, but I've done a lot of crucifixions in my day. This guy was dead.

ROBBY: You're sure?

MARCUS: I'm telling you, the guy bought the farm—and the back forty acres too!

ROBBY: I see. You also told me you were present the morning the tomb was found empty.

MARCUS: That's right. I had guard duty on the graveyard shift. *[Pause]* Uh, sorry. [Pause] I, um, had guard duty Saturday night through Sunday morning.

ROBBY: And during that time did you see anyone in the area other than the other guards?

MARCUS: Nope. It was pretty dead around there. *[Pause]* Uh, sorry.

ROBBY: When exactly did you realize the tomb was empty?

MARCUS: When one of the other guys said, "Hey, who moved the stone?"

ROBBY: The huge stone over the mouth of the tomb was moved, and none of you heard it or saw it? How'd that happen?

MARCUS: Um, well, the official story is we were asleep.

ROBBY: You must be *very* heavy sleepers!

MARCUS: We don't sleep on duty! That'll get you the death penalty!

ROBBY: Tough employer.

MARCUS: You're telling me.

ROBBY: Well, what happened then?

MARCUS: Just between you and me, there was this incredible earthquake, and this person—a bright, almost glowing, being—came down out of the sky. I was so scared I couldn't move. I was literally frozen in my sandals!

ROBBY: So why the "I fell asleep" story?

MARCUS: The chief priests offered us big bucks and promised to keep us out of trouble. Unlike you. Come on; we're going downtown. *[Grabs Robby's arm and starts ushering him off]* You have the right to remain silent . . .

ROBBY: *[Speaking over soldier reading him his rights]* This is Robby Rabbi reporting for channel 12 news. Susana.

SUSANA: Robby. Finally, tonight, another exclusive interview, this time with prize-winning reporter Mary Marry. Mary?

MARY: Susana. *[Pause]*

SUSANA: Don't even start with me.

MARY: Huh? *[To "camera"]* Good evening. I'm in the home of Mary Magdalene. If you recall, we interviewed Mary last week when she told us of having encountered the risen Jesus live and in person. Is that correct, Mary?

MARY2: It sure is, Mary.

MARY: Mary, I know you have more you want to tell us, but let's start by briefly going over the first week after the disappearance of Jesus' body.

MARY2: Disappearance? There was no disappearance. I'm telling you, I have seen Jesus and he's alive! I saw him in the garden outside the empty tomb, I saw him in Galilee when he appeared to his disciples, and I saw him when he appeared to a large crowd just yesterday.

MARY: You've been through a lot of stress and grief. Don't you suppose it's possible you just *thought* you saw Jesus?

MARY2: Don't give me all that silly psychobabble! I saw him, I touched him, and so did all the others. All of us couldn't have had the exact same hallucination at the exact same time. I'm telling you, he's alive!

MARY: *[Skeptically]* All righty then. Back to you, Susana.

MARY2: *[Grabs the microphone from Mary]* He's alive!

MARY: *[Begins a tug-of-war for the mike]* Susana?!

SUSANA: Thank you for that intriguing interview. Has Jesus really risen from the dead? This is one reporter who thinks it's worth looking into. *[♫ 19–theme music]* For everyone at the Nazareth Nightly News, I'm Susana Joanna. Good night.

[Susana stacks and straightens her papers. Lights dim if possible.]

Hints

Use your staging area creatively. We used the baptismal, which is located high behind the platform, for the upper room and actually draped a knotted bedsheet over the side to make it look like Robby had climbed up it to get inside. (Always check with the appropriate people about using sanctuary fixtures as props and staging.) We put the anchor desk stage L on the platform and created a living room scene stage R for the Mary/Mary2 interview. The Annas interview was done on the floor level DL. (See "Use Your Space" on page 16 for other ideas.)

This is an easy skit for sound if you have enough microphones. Instead of giving the reporters fake mikes to interview with, give them the real thing. There's no need to worry about projecting voices as long as the reporters remember to hold the mike out when the interviewee is speaking.

Check out "More Players than Parts" on page 15 and "Too Many Parts, Not Enough Players" on page 14 in the introduction for some ideas for incorporating more people or making do with only four actors in this sketch.

Discussion Questions

1. If today's media personalities were covering the story of the resurrection, whom do you think they'd choose to interview? What overall feeling do you think would be conveyed?

2. If it were possible to send the best investigative news team of today back in time to investigate the empty tomb of Jesus, do you think they'd return to tell us Jesus had really risen from the dead? Why or why not?

3. Why do you think there continues to be so much controversy over the resurrection of Jesus?

4. Throughout history people have tried to come up with plausible explanations for the empty tomb of Jesus other than his resurrection. Why do you think that is?

Pew Ponderings

THEME: Sometimes we allow our own critical spirit to get in the way of God's Holy Spirit.

SETTING: Sunday morning service at a typical church. A pulpit or podium is at stage L facing stage R. Four short pews, or four rows of three chairs each, face the pulpit. These should be on an angle to make players more easily seen by the audience.

CHARACTERS: Narrator who isn't seen onstage (Narr), Pastor, five congregation members (P1, P2, P3, P4, P5). A mix of genders and ages is advised for the congregation members, although P5 must be female, and P3 would probably be more effective as a male. (If your church expects women to wear dresses or skirts, do not cast a female as P4, as this player will be upside-down in a pew.) All other parts may be played by males or females.

COSTUMES: Dress clothes appropriate for Sunday morning service.

PROPS: Hymnals, Bible in a Bible cover with several Sunday school papers and a church newsletter inside.

(From Laura L. Martinez, *Drama for the Dramatically Challenged: Church Plays Made Easy* © 2000 by Judson Press. Reproduced by permission.)

[Note: Congregation members' voices are heard over the sound system to give the illusion of hearing their thoughts. Pastor's lines are delivered live.]

[🎧 20–optional voice-over of Narr's dialogue]

NARR: What if it were possible to hear the thoughts of those sitting in the pews on Sunday morning?

[🎧 21–organ chords]

[All players are standing with hymnals in hand. The last chords are heard on the organ as the players sing "Amen."]

PASTOR: Please be seated. *[Congregation sits]* What an inspiring hymn . . . *[Pastor's voice drifts off though actor appears to continue to "speak" throughout the remainder of the sketch]*

P1: Inspiring?! I have no idea what I just sang. What does "Here I raise my Ebenezer" mean? And what would that Scrooge guy from *A Christmas Carol* have to do with *[Reading from the hymnal]* "Come, Thou Fount of Every Blessing" anyway?

[🎧 22–laughter]

[P2, P3, P4 laugh with voice-over, but in a subdued manner]

P1: What? What's so funny? Oh man, I missed a good joke. The only part of the service I do find inspiring, and I missed it!

P2: *[Looks up from reading Sunday school paper]* Oh no, it's only the first joke of the sermon and I'm already halfway through my Sunday school paper. I read the church newsletter last week. What am I going to do for the rest of the message? I could write to someone. Do I have any paper? *[Starts rifling through Bible case. P1 turns to see what P2 is doing. P2 stops, embarrassed. They smile at each other. P1 turns back around.]* Oops. Well, no paper. Maybe if I read *really* slow I can make it last 'til the end of the sermon.

P3: *[P3 began slowly sinking lower and lower in pew soon after being seated. He is now slouched down, with head back and mouth open. Light snoring sounds are heard–recorded or live– and then a loud snort that startles P3 into a rigid sitting position. Looks around sheepishly.]* Oh man, I wonder if anyone heard that. *[Looks at Pastor]* I wonder if *he* heard that. Oh well, it's his fault anyway. If he'd just try to be a little more interesting . . . I mean, come on, tell me something I don't know. *[Yawns]* Maybe I should have gone to bed a little earlier. That was a good movie though . . . *[He has gradually returned to his original position and now drifts back off to sleep]*

P4: Bored. Bored . . . bored . . . bored. *[As these first four words are heard, P4 sinks onto back and then into an upside-down position with head hanging off the pew and feet over the back of the pew]* This is it. This is the week it kills me. My obituary will read, "Promising young student bored to death in church." I wonder if you still get to go to heaven when you die of boredom in church. I can just see myself standing in front of the pearly gates and Saint Peter saying, "What are you doing here? You're early!" "Yeah," I'll say, "I went to church this morning." I wonder if they let you in for that. *[Sits up abruptly]* Better not take any chances.

P5: *[Straining to see someone in a pew ahead of her]* I can't believe she wore that. Somebody needs to give that girl a fashion lesson. Maybe I'll casually mention my Tuesday shopping fellowship group and invite her to come along. The girls and I could drop a few subtle hints. *[Looks again]* OK, maybe not so subtle.

[♫ 23–optional music for altar call]

PASTOR: Please don't hesitate. The altar is open.

[All players sit up and appear to watch people walk past them to the altar]

P3: Is it time to go? *[Starts to get up]*

PASTOR: Let's respond together to God's Spirit.

P3: *[Sits back down]* Oops!

P4: What is everybody doing? What's going on?

P2: It must have been a salvation message. *[Strains to see who has gone to the altar]* I knew she wasn't saved! Wait, there's Mrs. Martin. She led me to the Lord when I was eight. What is every-body doing?

P5: *[Watching someone passing her on the way to the altar]* Those shoes do not go with that dress!

P1: Wow, I've never seen anything like this before. Half the church is up there. What's going on? *Did I miss something?*

Alterations

Like the narrator, the pastor could be unseen, with his or her voice also being heard over the sound system.

The lines for the above characters could be slightly altered for various audiences. For instance, if this sketch is being presented at a youth event, P3 could have stayed up late to watch *Saturday Night Live* or some other program popular with young people. Pronouns in the dialogue may also need to be changed depending on the gender of particular players—to allow for a female pastor, for example.

If your church does not print a newsletter, P2 could say, "I already read the bulletin announcements during Sunday school," instead of the line about having read the newsletter last week.

Hints

This is a great skit for adding extra people. Some could go forward for the altar call. Additional pew ponderers could be added with thoughts that address other issues that distract us on Sunday mornings. A worship leader could appear to be leading the hymn as the piece opens and then could follow the last chord with something like, "Great singing. Please be seated." He or she could then be seated behind the pastor stage L or in the congregation stage R (depending on your church's tradition). The pastor could then begin with, "What an inspiring hymn . . ." If your platform space is limited, be careful not to crowd people and props. You want all the players to be seen.

To keep the audience's attention focused on the appropriate character, have all players remain completely still unless their thoughts are the ones being heard. The pastor should appear to continue preaching, but his or her actions should be very limited so as not to attract undue attention. The pastor should also cheat in so his or her face is turned slightly away from the audience. (When I played this part, I simply read silently from the hymnal, occasionally lifting my head slightly to look at my congregation of actors. Just be sure the person playing this part is careful not to lose track of the movement through the script and forget to say the pastor's lines near the end.)

Have those playing the pastor and P3 write a complete sentence for their lines that fade out. The words they add should hardly be audible, and the sentences do not have to be completely spoken, but this will help them to appear more natural.

If possible, arrange to have someone familiar with your church sound system come to a rehearsal to record the actors' lines. The more professional the recording, the better quality the presentation. Have actors read more slowly than normal, and be sure to leave pauses of at least five full seconds between each person's part. Try to anticipate where your audience will laugh, and allow for appropriate pauses on the tape so they will not miss the next line. If the pastor is going to appear on the stage, be sure to leave enough time for the pastor's lines between the others' lines at the end of the piece.

It is very important that you rehearse several times with the tape once it is made. This gives your sound person a chance to get used to coordinating your tape with the special effects CD (if you choose to use the latter along with your recorded parts). Though it may sound easier to act without having to recite lines, it is actually a bit harder. Help your actors come up with enough stage business to do and encourage them to overact slightly, both with facial expressions and with movements.

Discussion Questions

1. Which of these characters can you most relate to and why?

2. Who is to blame for the characters' boredom?

3. What do you think God would want each of these characters to do in the future?

4. Besides trying to pay attention, what other actions might these characters take?

Playing House

THEME: The God of the universe became human in every way, beginning as a helpless infant.

SETTING: Church sanctuary or other location where a drama team will be rehearsing for an upcoming presentation.

CHARACTERS: Two females (F1, F2) and two males (M1, M2), all at least of senior high age; Director (D), preferably adult.

PROPS: A script of the reading portion of this sketch for each player (preferably in a black three-ring binder), a nativity set (with large pieces if possible) set up on a table or some type of stand.

[F1 is moving some of the nativity pieces, engrossed in her silent game of "house." M1 enters down center aisle.]

M1: What ya doin'?

F1: Just having a little fun while I wait for the rest of the drama team to show up for rehearsal.

M1: *[Patronizing]* Ohhhh.

F1: Didn't you ever play with the nativity set as a kid?

M1: Nope. Must be a girl thing.

F1: Oh, come on, live a little. *[Picks up a wise man]* "Excuse us, ma'am, we've come to see the baby."

M1: *[Moves the sheep]* Baaaa.

(From Laura L. Martinez, *Drama for the Dramatically Challenged: Church Plays Made Easy* © 2000 by Judson Press. Reproduced by permission.)

F1: We've brought gifts for him.

M1: Moooo.

F1: Gold. Frankincense. And myrrh.

M1: What do camels say?

F1: What is it with guys and sound effects?

[On this last line M2 and F2 enter down center aisle]

F2: Oooo, can I play?

M2: Play what?

F1,2: Nativity.

M1: *[To M2]* It's a girl thing.

F1: You can do Mary and Joseph.

F2: Cool!

[F2 and M2 join in the play]

M1: Hee-haw, hee-haw.

M2: Moooo.

[F1 and F2 exchange looks of disgust. The barn noises get louder. M1 wiggles the manger.]

M1: Whaaaa.

F1: *[Shocked]* What are you doing?

M1: The animals woke up the baby.

F1: But that's baby Jesus!

M2: So?

F1: He doesn't cry.

F2: Huh?

M1: How do you know that?

F1: It says so in the Bible: "The cattle are lowing, the poor baby wakes, but little Lord Jesus, no crying he makes."

F2: That's not in the Bible.

M2: That's a Christmas song.

F1: Bible, hymnal, whatever. We're talking the baby Jesus here.

M1: So you're saying he was like a superhuman baby—never cried, never wet his swaddling clothes?

F1: Well, I . . . I don't know. He was God.

F2: Yeah, God in the flesh.

[Director enters up center aisle, speaking as he or she comes]

D: OK, everybody, let's get right to Sunday's Advent reading.

[All take their places on the platform; the following portion is read from players' script folders]

[⌖ 24–optional music]

M2: And the Word became flesh and lived among us, and we have seen his glory, the glory as of a father's only son, full of grace and truth.

M1: Christ Jesus, though he was in the form of God, did not regard equality with God as something to be exploited, but emptied himself, taking the form of a slave, being born in human likeness.

F2: Now the birth of Jesus the Messiah took place in this way. When his mother Mary had been engaged to Joseph, but before they lived together, she was found to be with child from the Holy Spirit.

M1: Her husband Joseph, being a righteous man and unwilling to expose her to public disgrace, planned to dismiss her quietly.

F1: But just when he had resolved to do this, an angel of the Lord appeared to him in a dream and said,

M2: "Joseph, son of David, do not be afraid to take Mary as your wife, for the child conceived in her is from the Holy Spirit. She will bear a son, and you are to name him Jesus, for he will save his people from their sins."

F1: All this took place to fulfill what had been spoken by the Lord through the prophet:

M1: "Look, the virgin shall conceive and bear a son, and they shall name him Emmanuel," which means, "God is with us."

F1: The Creator of the universe chose to be born.

F2: Born in a dirty stable.

M2: Among dirty animals.

M1: Visited by dirty shepherds.

F2: He came willingly to a dark and dirty world.

F1: To be like us.

F2: To live with us.

M2: In all the messiness of humanity.

ALL: We believe

F2: in one Lord Jesus Christ,

M1: the only-begotten Son of God,

F1: begotten of the Father before all worlds,

M2: God of God,

M1: Light of Light,

F2: Very God of Very God,

M1: begotten, not made,

F2: being of one substance with the Father,

M2: by whom all things were made;

F1: who for us and for our salvation, came down from heaven,

M1: and was incarnate by the Holy Spirit of the Virgin Mary,

ALL: and was made man.

[Music fades]

D: Good job, you guys. I've got to run a few copies before we rehearse our next piece, so go ahead and take a five-minute break.

[All exit except F1 (director down center aisle, others anywhere). F1 X to nativity scene.]

F1: *[Picking up baby Jesus]* And was made man. *[Looks up]* God in the flesh.

NOTE: Scripture references from the New Revised Standard Version, in order of appearance: John 1:14; Philippians 2:5–7; Matthew 1:18–23. Also quoted: the Nicene Creed.

Alterations

If the location of your rehearsals/performance does not normally have a nativity scene set up or if you are presenting this piece at a time other than Christmas, you will need to add a line at the beginning to explain the presence of a nativity set. For example:

M1: *[Entering]* Hi.

F1: Hi. Look what I found. Someone must have found this during the church cleanup yesterday.

M1: What are you doing with it?

Continue from here with F1's first line in the original script.

The phrases "drama team" and "Sunday's Advent reading" may need to be modified to fit your specific situation.

Hints

Following this sketch with the song "Emmanuel," written by Bob McGee (C. A. Music, 1976), adds a special time of contemplation and worship.

We used this piece in place of a traditional Advent reading and followed it with the lighting of the Advent candle.

Discussion Questions

1. Why do we sometimes have a hard time thinking of Jesus as being human in every way?

2. What aspect of Jesus' humanness do you find most amazing and why?

3. How do you feel when you think about the Creator of the universe becoming human?

4. Why is it important for us to reflect on the Incarnation?

The Valentine

THEME: Our intentional acts of kindness may someday point someone to Christ.

SETTING: First half—a children's school classroom on Valentine's Day; second half—an AA meeting about eighteen years later.

CHARACTERS: A teacher (can be a voice only) and six students: Ronny, Becky, Ginger, Brenda, Pete, and Kyle (could substitute females for Pete and Kyle if necessary). In the first half, the students are in the third grade. All six play adults in the second half of the sketch. All parts should be played by actors of senior-high age or older.

COSTUMES: Street clothes are fine, but try to add accessories that give the illusion of childhood and that can be easily removed for the second half of this piece: hair ribbons, baseball caps, etc. A jacket or other adult-looking pieces of clothing could be added for the second half. Young Ronny should be dressed to look poor and unkempt. Again, this appearance needs to be easily "fixed" for the second half.

PROPS: Six lunch bags decorated with hearts, etc.; several markers; six chairs arranged in two rows (small desks or chairs with desktops attached would be ideal); several store-bought valentines (or just the small white envelopes) for kids to exchange; three or four homemade hearts with crayon writing on them (they should be distinct from the commercial cards and have no envelopes); a very large and elaborately decorated heart valentine and another one just like it that looks old and worn; wastebasket; small podium (optional).

(From Laura L. Martinez, *Drama for the Dramatically Challenged: Church Plays Made Easy* © 2000 by Judson Press. Reproduced by permission.)

[The scene opens with the children in their seats decorating their Valentine bags with markers. The children are seated as follows: front row, right to left–Ronny, Pete, Ginger; back row, right to left– Kyle, Brenda, Becky.]

[🎧 25–optional music]

GINGER: Becky, can I have the red marker when you're done with it?

BECKY: Sure. *[Hands it to her]* Here.

GINGER: Thanks.

PETE: Hey Ronny, what are you wasting your time for? You're not gonna get any valentines.

KYLE: Yeah, who would pay good money to give you one? *[To Pete]* It would probably just disintegrate when he touched it!

[The two have a good laugh together as the teacher enters or voice begins to speak from offstage]

[🎧 26–optional Teacher voice-over]

TEACHER: OK, class, it's time to exchange our valentines.

[Children pick up their valentines and begin exchanging. Ronny X L to Ginger and gives her a card.]

GINGER: Uh . . . thanks, Ronny. Umm . . . *[She rummages through her cards and then crosses her name off the valentine Ronny has just given her and writes his name on it]*

GINGER: *[As she writes]* To Ronny. *[Hands it to him]* Here you are.

RONNY: *[Confused and disappointed]* Thanks.

[Ronny X DC to Brenda, who has stepped DC to put a valentine on Pete's desk. Ronny hands her a valentine. She takes it as if it's infected with the plague and X L to Ginger. They giggle, and she discards the valentine in the wastebasket DL. Unbeknownst to them, Ronny has seen it all, and he returns to his seat dejected. By now Pete and Kyle are stage R, and they nudge each other knowingly as they watch Ronny. Becky approaches Ronny with a large heart card.]

BECKY: Happy Valentine's Day, Ronny. *[Gives him the card]*

GIRLS: Ooooooooo!

PETE: *[Singing]* Becky loves Ronny.

RONNY: It's OK, Becky. Just say I gave it to you, and you're giving it back.

BECKY: No, Ronny, I worked on this for an hour last night, and I want you to have it.

RONNY: You do? *[Becky nods]* Why?

[All actors freeze for a mental count of three seconds.]

[👂 27–music]

[While transition music plays, actors snap into action rearranging the chairs in two rows, three chairs deep, facing stage R. "Costume" changes are made, and Ronny's appearance is cleaned up. He stands at a small podium L facing the others now seated in chairs. When music fades, he begins to speak.]

RONNY: Hi. My name is Ron, and I'm an alcoholic.

ALL: Hi, Ron.

RONNY: Today is my one-year sobriety birthday.

[All applaud]

RONNY: Thank you. Uh, I grew up in a home where alcohol was a normal part of life. My mother was often drunk, and I had to learn to fend for myself. My dad left us when I was only five. I was never very well liked. Most of my school years were filled with teasing and abuse. I grew up thinking I was worthless. I started drinking at age thirteen. Alcohol was easy to get ahold of, and it seemed to take the edge off the hurt. Before I knew it, I was drinking more and more, getting into trouble at home and school. I dropped out of school at sixteen, and my mom kicked me out at seventeen. I worked odd jobs to support my drinking. I was what I'd always thought I'd be–nothing.

Then one day I was packing up what little I had after being evicted–again. And this *[Holds up the old valentine]* fell out of a box. It's a valentine I got in the third grade. It was the only one I got. Anyway, I decided to see if I could find the girl who gave it to me. I went back to my old neighborhood. Her parents still lived in that same big old house. They told me Becky died in a car accident only a month earlier. They invited me in, and we talked. They showed me Becky's obituary. Part of it said, "Becky Roberts will always be remembered by family and friends as someone who loved the unlovely. She lived life by the motto 'Show others God's love by loving them yourself.'"

And suddenly I knew why Becky gave me that valentine. She wanted me to know Someone loved me, that I mattered. I wasn't worthless, and I didn't have to live like I was. God loves me, and I am somebody. Thanks, Becky. Happy Valentine's Day.

Hints

When placing the chairs for both scenes, stagger them so the back row can be more easily seen. Even though this is not "true to life," it is acceptable staging. Another option would be to place the scene on an angle. The AA meeting could also be set up with the actors seated in profile or with the group's backs to the audience and Ronny facing out C, since Ronny is the only one the audience needs to see. Depending on the depth of your stage area, you may need to go to two rows deep and three chairs wide to do the latter. Set your stage with the audience in mind. You want visibility as well as realism.

If you have access to only a few school desks, set them in the front row and use chairs alone in the back row. This still gives the illusion of a classroom.

While exchanging valentines, players should not travel too far. You want to avoid drawing attention away from Ronny. If two players exchange more than once or if Pete never gives a card to Ginger, no one is going to notice. Suggest various stage-business ideas to help players look convincing without a lot of traveling (for example, shuffling cards to find the right one to give, putting cards in bag and looking in to see how many have been received, taking one out of its envelope and reading it.)

Rehearse the resetting of the stage between the two scenes to ensure a quick and smooth transition. It is important that this action does not break the mood of the piece. The entire change, including costuming, should take no more than forty-five seconds.

Ron's speech in the second half of the sketch can be read. (Be sure to enlarge the print so it is easier to read.) He should not sound too rehearsed—there should be a feeling of his being uncomfortable. Actions such as shifting his weight, clearing his throat, etc., are appropriate as long as they appear natural and are not overdone.

Discussion Questions

1. Most of us aren't outwardly cruel, as were the first two kids. More often we are just thoughtless, as was the girl who "recycled" a card for Ronny. Think of some examples of "careless cruelty" someone your age might do.

2. The girl who threw Ronny's valentine away didn't think he was watching. In what ways do our unkind acts hurt people even if they don't witness it directly?

3. Do you think it's OK if we pretend to be nice to someone when we're with him or her but don't really mean it? Why or why not?

4. Think about the Ronnys in your life. Without naming names, brainstorm as many ways as possible that you can demonstrate God's love to them.

5. What might following through with these ideas cost you? What might you receive?

Virtuous Woman

THEME: The Proverbs 31 woman is given, not as a standard of perfection, but as a principle of caring diligently for the needs of one's family.

SETTING: The narrator stands DL at a podium. If the action will take place on a raised platform that is easily accessible from the floor, place the narrator on the floor level. The main stage should be set with the various props spread out so as to create some distance between each "station." Stations are (1) table with utensils, lunch box, food basket, etc.; (2) table with sewing machine, lamp, fabric, and calculator; (3) aerobics step and weights; (4) gardening tools. If possible, the cookie sheet and oven mitt should be offstage, requiring the Virtuous Woman to leave the stage to retrieve them.

CHARACTERS: Female narrator (Narr), Virtuous Woman (VW).

COSTUMES: Typical Sunday church attire for both women. Additional accessories for VW: a stretchy headband (at first it is just to hold her hair; later it becomes a sweatband), a watch, and an apron.

PROPS: Podium, large lunch box, lunch items, apple, two candy bars, several pieces of fabric, measuring tape, small table with bowls and utensils, clipboard and pen, oven mitt, cookie sheet, gardening gloves or a sun hat, small gardening spade and rake, two small dumbbells, an aerobics step, large calculator or an adding machine, small lamp and a sewing machine (both connected to a power supply if possible), stand or small table for lamp and sewing machine, chair, small wicker basket containing canned goods and fruit, a child's red sweatshirt or jacket, woman's blouse

(From Laura L. Martinez, *Drama for the Dramatically Challenged: Church Plays Made Easy* © 2000 by Judson Press. Reproduced by permission.)

(not purple), something purple (jacket, dress, etc.) that would fit VW or just a large piece of purple fabric, box or basket with the words "For Sale" on the side

---

[As the reading begins, VW enters humming and almost flitting about as she acts out the passage. As the reading progresses, however, she becomes less cheerful and more harried. Narr reads slowly, with a sense of joy and pride.]

NARR: A reading from Proverbs 31:

[♫ 28–optional music]

A virtuous woman who can find? She is far more precious than jewels.

[VW begins packing husband's lunch]

The heart of her husband trusts in her, and he will have no lack of gain.

[VW puts in two candy bars]

She does him good, and not harm, all the days of her life.

[Takes out one candy bar and puts in an apple]

She seeks wool and flax, and works with willing hands.

[Sits at sewing machine, puts measuring tape around neck, and picks up fabric ready to sew]

She is like the ships of the merchant, she brings her food from far away.

[She jumps up and heads offstage, then hurries back with tray of imaginary cookies and places them on food table]

She rises while it is still night and provides food for her household

[Yawns and stirs something]

and tasks for her servant girls.

[Picks up clipboard and jots a note]

She considers a field and buys it; with the fruit of her hands she plants a vineyard.

[Rushes to put on gardening gloves or sun hat, picks up tools, and starts to exit]

She girds herself with strength, and makes her arms strong.

[Quickly ditches the hat and tools, pulls down her headband to make it a sweatband, picks up weights, and begins lifting them and stepping on and off the aerobics step]

She perceives that her merchandise is profitable. Her lamp does not
  go out at night.

[Drops weights. Goes to calculator and begins adding numbers. Yawns and turns on lamp.]

She puts her hands to the distaff,

[Could have her look confused and mouth, "Distaff?" and then resolve it with the next line. Or just have this flow right into the next line's action.]

and her hands hold the spindle.

[Returns to sit at sewing machine]

She opens her hand to the poor, and reaches out her hands to the
  needy.

[Rushes to table and begins adding food to the food basket]

She is not afraid for her household when it snows,

[Back to sewing machine]

for all her household are clothed in crimson.

[Holds up a red article of warm clothing and then acts as if she will begin mending it at the machine]

She makes herself coverings;

[Throws the above clothing and searches through fabric]

her clothing is fine linen

[Begins to put on blouse that is not purple]

and purple.

[Removes and throws blouse and continues searching]

Her husband is known in the city gates, taking his seat among the
  elders of the land.

[Finds something purple–whether clothing or just cloth–and puts it on in a haphazard manner]

She makes linen garments and sells them; she supplies the merchant
  with sashes.

[Begins stuffing fabric in box and places it on table with "For Sale" clearly visible]

Strength and dignity are her clothing,

[She stands, looking bedraggled]

and she laughs at the time to come.

[She begins chuckling. The chuckle becomes out-and-out laughter. The background music stops abruptly—not a fade. During this time, Narr has turned back and opened her mouth as if to continue reading but stops to look back at VW a couple of times. Finally she gives up and turns to VW.]

NARR: *[Embarrassed]* What are you doing?

VW: *[Still laughing]* A virtuous woman who can find? *[Becoming angry]* Is that a rhetorical question? There's no such thing!

NARR: Don't yell at me. I'm just reading the verses.

VW: And I'm just acting them out, and it's killing me!

NARR: What are you saying? It can't be done?

VW: *[X DL]* Listen, unless the fine linen she wore was a blue leotard with a red cape . . . *[Thoughtful pause]* I don't know about you, but I can't do all those things—not and do them all well. *[She sits, possibly on the edge of the platform or altar rail]*

NARR: *[Dejected]* Yeah, *[Joins VW]* me neither.

[The next several lines are delivered out and over the heads of the audience rather than to each other. This will convey the idea that the women are lost in thought as they process these ideas.]

VW: Every Mother's Day somebody reads that Scripture. And every Mother's Day I feel guilty that I don't measure up.

[They sit in silence for a moment]

VW: Ya know, I have a good friend that's a pretty admirable woman.

NARR: Yeah?

VW: Yeah. She's involved in ministry, and she keeps the needs of her family as her main priority. She hasn't purchased a field lately.

NARR: There's a lady in my church I think of as pretty virtuous. She prays for others in need, loves her family, and has a close connection to God. I don't think she sells sashes to the merchants, but . . .

VW: Now that I think about it, my mom is a Proverbs 31 woman. She never had servant girls, but she always had a list of chores for us kids. She made personal sacrifices to meet our needs. And more than once she burned the midnight oil to take care of us.

NARR: Maybe there's hope for us?

VW: Maybe. What if it's more about doing what we can instead of about doing everything?

NARR: Yeah, and about loving God and our family and serving them out of that love, not out of a need to meet standards of perfection.

[They smile at each other. Woman stands.]

VW: Just call me Virtuous Woman. *[Strikes a Superman pose]*

NARR: *[Stands]* And her sidekick Veronica. *[Also strikes a pose]*

[VW looks at her with a confused look]

NARR: *[Sheepishly]* I always liked the name Veronica.

[VW shrugs]

BOTH: A virtuous woman who can find?

*[☞ **29**–optional superhero music]*

NARR: *[Pointing up and out]* It's a maid . . .

VW: *[Also pointing]* It's a teacher . . .

NARR: *[Points in new direction]* It's a nurse . . .

VW: It's a wife . . .

NARR: It's a friend . . .

VW: It's a mom . . .

NARR: No, it's . . .

[Music stops before last line]

VW: *[Takes a step forward]* just me–and Veronica!

Hints

The beginning script is simply Proverbs 31:10–25. It can be read from any translation; however, it is suggested that the King James Version for verse 10a be used: "Who can find a virtuous woman?" or "A virtuous woman who can find?" Otherwise the ending will need to be altered to fit your version's text. The script above is taken from the New Revised Standard Version.

The reading of Proverbs 31 should be smooth (even though the script makes it look fragmented). Narr should not look to the stage to make sure that VW is getting where she needs to go. Instead this piece should be well rehearsed to work out the proper speed of the reading.

If Narr's podium will be blocking a clear view for some of the audience when the women sit, have Narr move it as she goes to sit next to VW.

Use caution on the aerobics step if you are wearing dress shoes. This can be a slippery combination. (I almost broke my neck in the original performance of this piece!)

Discussion Questions

1. Do you think the writer of Proverbs 31 was describing a real person? Why or why not?

2. What is the difference between a pattern and a role model? Which do you think the Proverbs 31 woman was meant to be and why?

3. What admirable qualities do you see in the Proverbs 31 woman?

4. Which of these qualities have you seen in your mom or someone who has been like a mom to you?

5. Which admirable qualities of the Proverbs 31 woman would you like to strengthen in your own life?

The Weatherman Said

THEME: The world may look safe and calm, but God's Word warns us that our enemy prowls about and we must take precautions to be prepared for his attacks.

SETTING: The breakfast table, just before school and work.

CHARACTERS: Mom, Dad, Brent (a child about eight years old; could be female–Brenda), Reader.

COSTUMES: Mom can wear most anything, even a bathrobe and slippers would be fine. Dad should be dressed in a dress shirt and tie, preferably one that will show wetness well. Brent wears school clothes and will also need a raincoat, boots, and a rain hat. (We used a rain poncho and just altered the lines a bit; that is, "hat" became "hood.")

PROPS: Small table with three chairs, bowls, spoons, cups, cereal box, milk jug, pitcher, kitchen towel, backpack, pair of kid's shoes, pen, note, umbrella, optional "window" (see "Need a Window?" on page 16), pitcher of water, tarp, small wading pool. (Last three items are offstage.)

(From Laura L. Martinez, *Drama for the Dramatically Challenged: Church Plays Made Easy* © 2000 by Judson Press. Reproduced by permission.)

[Family is sitting at the table finishing the morning meal. Mom is writing a note.]

MOM: When you drop Brent off at school, be sure to give him this note for his teacher.

DAD: *[Takes the note, hands it to Brent]* Here, give this to your teacher.

BRENT: *[Takes note]* OK.

MOM: *[Retrieves note and gives it back to Dad]* No, no. You have to wait 'til the last minute, or he'll forget.

DAD: *[Takes note and slips it in pocket]* OK, but who's gonna remind me? *[Gets up]* Come on, Brent; we're gonna be late.

BRENT: *[Gets up and follows Dad to L]* OK.

MOM: *[To Brent]* Wear your boots. The weatherman said it's gonna rain.

BRENT: OK. *[Puts his boots on and puts his shoes in his backpack]*

MOM: *[To Dad]* You might want to wear your sneakers and carry your good shoes. It's supposed to be a downpour.

DAD: That's crazy. It's a beautiful, sunny day. Let's go, Brent.

BRENT: OK.

[They start to exit]

MOM: Hold on; let's get that raincoat on. The weatherman said the rain will start first thing this morning.

BRENT: OK. *[He puts on his raincoat]*

MOM: *[To Dad]* Why don't you take your overcoat?

DAD: Honey, I appreciate the concern, but it's not gonna rain. Just look outside. Do you see any ominous signs, dark rain clouds, anything?

MOM: Well, no, but the weatherman said . . .

DAD: Weathermen can be wrong.

MOM: I don't know. This one is usually right on the money.

DAD: We're gonna be late. Come on, Brent.

BRENT: OK.

MOM: *[To Brent]* Just a minute. Put on your hat. You don't want to sit in the classroom with a wet head all morning.

BRENT: OK.

MOM: *[To Dad]* You should at least take an umbrella . . .

[She holds umbrella out to him. He begins to protest.]

DAD: Susan . . .

MOM: Just in case.

DAD: Fine. I'll use it as shade from the bright sunlight!

[Takes umbrella, and he and son exit L]

MOM: Bye. Have a wonderful day. *[X to C. Picks up towel, throws it over her shoulder, and begins clearing table]*

*[👂 **30**–thunder and rain]*

[After a brief moment, Dad enters with umbrella partially open but pointing down as if he were frozen in the motion of opening it. He is dripping wet (due to the fact that while he was offstage a stagehand poured the pitcher of water over his head). Brent follows trying to stifle laughter.]

MOM: *[Takes towel from shoulder]* Towel? *[Tosses it to him]*

[Actors freeze while Scripture is read]

READER: *[Stands DC on audience level]* Discipline yourselves, keep alert. Like a roaring lion your adversary the devil prowls around, looking for someone to devour.

Therefore take up the whole armor of God, so that you may be able to withstand on that evil day, and having done everything, to stand firm. Stand therefore, and fasten the belt of truth around your waist, and put on the breastplate of righteousness. As shoes for your feet put on whatever will make you ready to proclaim the gospel of peace. With all of these, take the shield of faith, with which you will be able to quench all the flaming arrows of the evil one. Take the helmet of salvation, and sword of the Spirit, which is the word of God. Pray in the Spirit at all times in every prayer and supplication. To that end keep alert.

NOTE: Scripture passages in order of appearance: 1 Peter 5:8; Ephesians 6:13–18, NRSV.

Alterations

The reader could be unseen, speaking in a microphone offstage, or use the voice-over provided on the companion CD (31). You might also replace the reader with a trio in a very simple readers' theater style (see "Readers' Theater" on page 12).

Hints

Make sure the offstage area is well protected with tarp, towels, etc. We made a makeshift shower stall around the wading pool, and the stagehand stood on steps above to pour the water on Dad. Any spills should be mopped up quickly and quietly by stagehands.

We used this skit to observe the International Day of Prayer for the Persecuted Church, which is observed the second Sunday of November. I introduced the skit with a few words regarding the tremendous persecution fellow believers face in other countries and how easy it is for us in America to become lax in our faith because the persecution we face is usually relatively mild. We need to be prepared, lest our enemy catch us unaware.

Kitchen towels are fairly light and can be hard to throw with any accuracy. Dampen it thoroughly and wring it out well just before the performance. This will allow Mom to be more likely to hit her target. Have her be careful not to let it hit Dad in his face though. This gives a rather comedic effect and distracts from the reading. It would be better to have it hit him and fall to the floor than to remain over his face.

Discussion Questions

1. What factors cause us to neglect putting on our spiritual armor?

2. Which piece of God's armor do you struggle with most and why?

3. What can Christians do to be more aware of their need for God's armor?

4. Can you think of a time in your own life when Satan caught you off guard?

Words from the Cross

THEME: An arrangement of Old and New Testament Scriptures on the theme of Christ's sacrificial death.

CHARACTERS: Four readers, preferably males for 1 and 2, females for 3 and 4.

COSTUMES, PROPS, SETTING: See "Readers' Theater" on page 12 in the introduction.

1: Who has believed our message and to whom has the arm of the LORD been revealed?

2: He grew up before him like a tender shoot, and like a root out of dry ground. He had no beauty or majesty to attract us to him, nothing in his appearance that we should desire him.

3: He was despised and rejected by men, a man of sorrows, and familiar with suffering.

1: Look, I am bringing him out to you to let you know that I find no basis for a charge against him. Here is the man.

2,3,4: Crucify, crucify!

1: You take him and crucify him. As for me, I find no basis for a charge against him.

4: We have a law, and according to that law, he must die because he claimed to be the Son of God.

1: What shall I do, then, with Jesus who is called Christ?

(From Laura L. Martinez, *Drama for the Dramatically Challenged: Church Plays Made Easy* © 2000 by Judson Press. Reproduced by permission.)

2,3,4: Away with him! Crucify! Crucify him!

1: Why? What crime has he committed?

2,3,4: Crucify him! Crucify!

[♫ **32**–*optional music*]

2: Surely he took up our infirmities and carried our sorrows, yet we considered him stricken by God, smitten by him, and afflicted.

4: But he was pierced for our transgressions, he was crushed for our iniquities; the punishment that brought us peace was upon him,

ALL: and by his wounds we are healed.

2,3,4: We all, like sheep, have gone astray,

3: each of us has turned to his own way;

2,3: and the LORD has laid on him the iniquity of us all.*

4: Then they led him out to crucify him.

2: When they came to the place called the Skull,

1,2: there they crucified him,

1,2,4: along with the criminals–

3: one on his right,

4: the other on his left.

2: Dogs have surrounded me; a band of evil men has encircled me, they have pierced my hands and feet. I can count all my bones; people stare and gloat over me.

1: If you are the king of the Jews, save yourself.

3: One of the criminals who hung there hurled insults at him:

4: Aren't you the Christ? Save yourself and us!

1: But the other criminal rebuked him:

3: Don't you fear God, since you are under the same sentence? We are punished justly, for we are getting what our deeds deserve. But this man has done nothing wrong. Jesus, remember me when you come into your kingdom.

2: I tell you the truth, today you will be with me in paradise.*

4: You brought me out of the womb; you made me trust in you even at my mother's breast. From birth I was cast upon you; from my mother's womb you have been my God. Do not be far from me, for trouble is near and there is no one to help.

2: I am poured out like water, and all my bones are out of joint. My heart has turned to wax; it has melted away within me. My strength is dried up . . . and my tongue sticks to the roof of my mouth; you lay me in the dust of death.*

3: At the sixth hour darkness came over the whole land until the ninth hour. At the ninth hour Jesus cried out in a loud voice,

2: My God, my God, why have you forsaken me?

4: My God, my God, why have you forsaken me? Why are you so far from saving me, so far from the words of my groaning? Oh my God, I cry out by day, but you do not answer, by night, and am not silent.

1: By oppression and judgment he was taken away. And who can speak of his descendants? For he was cut off from the land of the living; for the transgression of my people he was stricken.

2: Father, into your hands I commit my spirit. *[Pause]* It is finished.*

3: At the place where Jesus was crucified, there was a garden, and in the garden a new tomb, in which no one had ever been laid.

4: Because it was the Jewish day of Preparation and since the tomb was nearby, they laid Jesus there.

1: He was assigned a grave with the wicked, and with the rich in his death, though he had done no violence, nor was any deceit in his mouth.

2: Yet it was the LORD's will to crush him and cause him to suffer, and though the LORD makes his life a guilt offering, he will see his offspring and prolong his days, and the will of the LORD will prosper in his hand.

3: After the suffering of his soul,

3,4: he will see the light of life

3: and be satisfied;

4: by his knowledge my righteous servant will justify many, and he will bear their iniquities.*

1: You are enthroned as the Holy One;

ALL: you are the praise of Israel.

1: In you our fathers put their trust;

ALL: they trusted

1: and you delivered them.

2: They cried to you and were saved; in you they trusted and were not disappointed.

3: Therefore I will give him a portion among the great, and he will divide the spoils with the strong, because he poured out his life unto death, and was numbered with the transgressors. For he bore the sin of many, and made intercession for the transgressors.

ALL: God made him who had no sin to be sin for us, so that in him we might become the righteousness of God.

NOTE: Scripture references in biblical order: Psalm 22:1–17; Isaiah 53:1–12; Matthew 27:22–23; Mark 15:33–34; Luke 23:33,37,39–43; John 19:26–27,41–42; and 2 Corinthians 5:21, NIV.

Alterations

This piece could be altered for as few as three and as many as five readers. Three readers would be the bare minimum and will not have quite the same impact. More than five could become too busy and cumbersome.

Hints

The asterisks (*) in the script indicate a natural break in the reading, especially where there is a switch from Old to New Testament Scripture. These are places in the script where the audience will need help preparing mentally for a shift in thought or intensity of mood. This can be done by using one or more of the following techniques: a dramatic pause, a physical relocation by one or more readers, a changing of focal points (one or more actors turn their heads slightly and choose a new place on the back wall on which to fix their eyes), a few steps taken by the next reader as the next lines are begun (assuming there has been no movement with the preceding lines).

For other helps, please see "Readers' Theater" on page 12 in the introduction.

Discussion Questions

1. What stands out most in your mind after this reading?

2. What amazes you most about the crucifixion of Jesus?

3. Read 2 Corinthians 5:21 (the last line of this script) again. In light of the whole reading, how does this verse make you feel?

Words past the Tomb

THEME: An arrangement of New Testament passages about the resurrection of Jesus Christ.

CHARACTERS: Four readers, preferably males for 1 and 3, females for 2 and 4.

COSTUMES, PROPS, SETTING: See "Readers' Theater" on page 12 in the introduction.

[♫ 33–optional music]

1: Early on the first day of the week, while it was still dark, Mary Magdalene went to the tomb and saw that the stone had been removed from the entrance. So she came running to Simon Peter and the other disciple, the one Jesus loved.

2: They have taken the Lord out of the tomb, and we don't know where they have put him!

1: So Peter and the other disciple started for the tomb.

2,3: Both were running,

2: but the other disciple outran Peter and reached the tomb first. He bent over and looked in at the strips of linen lying there but did not go in. Then Simon Peter, who was behind him, arrived and went into the tomb. He saw the strips of linen lying there, as well as the burial cloth that had been around Jesus' head. The cloth was folded up by itself, separate from the linen. Finally the other

(From Laura L. Martinez, *Drama for the Dramatically Challenged: Church Plays Made Easy* © 2000 by Judson Press. Reproduced by permission.)

disciple, who had reached the tomb first, also went inside. He saw and believed.

4: They still did not understand from Scripture that Jesus had to rise from the dead.

2,3: Then the disciples went back to their homes,

1: but Mary stood outside the tomb crying. As she wept, she bent over to look into the tomb and saw two angels in white, seated where Jesus' body had been,

4: one at the head

3: and the other at the foot.

1: Woman, why are you crying?

2: They have taken my Lord away, and I don't know where they have put him.

4: At this, she turned around and saw Jesus standing there, but she did not realize that it was Jesus.

1: Woman, why are you crying? Who is it you are looking for?

3: Thinking he was the gardener, she said,

2: Sir, if you have carried him away, tell me where you have put him, and I will get him.

1: Mary.

2: Teacher!

1: Do not hold on to me, for I have not yet returned to the Father. Go instead to my brothers and tell them, I am returning to my Father and your Father, to my God and your God.

3: Mary Magdalene went to the disciples with the news:

2: I have seen the Lord!

4: And she told them that he had said these things to her.

1: On the evening of that first day of the week, when the disciples were together, with the doors locked for fear of the Jews, Jesus came and stood among them.

3: Peace be with you!

1,2: They were startled and

1,2,4: frightened,

2: thinking they saw a ghost.

3: Why are you troubled, and why do doubts rise in your minds? Look at my hands and my feet. It is I myself! Touch me and see; a ghost does not have flesh and bones, as you see I have.

1: He showed them his hands and feet.

2,4: The disciples were overjoyed.

3: Peace be with you! As the Father has sent me, I am sending you.

1: And with that he breathed on them.

3: Receive the Holy Spirit.

4: Now Thomas,

1: one of the Twelve,

4: was not with the disciples when Jesus came.

2: So the other disciples told him,

ALL: We have seen the Lord!

1: Unless I see the nail marks in his hands and put my finger where the nails were, and put my hand into his side, I will not believe it.

2: A week later his disciples were in the house again,

4: and Thomas was with them.

2: Though the doors were locked, Jesus came and stood among them.

3: Peace be with you!

2: Then he said to Thomas,

3: Put your finger here; see my hands. Reach out your hand and put it into my side. Stop doubting and believe.

1: My Lord and my God!

3: Because you have seen me, you have believed; blessed are those who have not seen and yet have believed.

1,4: Now faith is being sure of what we hope for and certain of what we do not see.

3: This is what I told you while I was still with you: Everything must be fulfilled that is written about me in the Law of Moses, the Prophets and the Psalms.

4: Then he opened their minds so they could understand the Scriptures.

3: This is what is written: The Christ will suffer and rise from the dead on the third day, and repentance and forgiveness of sins will be preached in his name to all nations, beginning at Jerusalem. You are witnesses of these things. I am going to send you what my Father has promised; but stay in the city until you have been clothed with power from on high.

2: When he had led them out to the vicinity of Bethany, he lifted up his hands and blessed them. While he was blessing them, he left them and was taken up into heaven. Then they worshiped him and returned to Jerusalem with great joy. And they stayed continually at the temple,

ALL: praising God.

4: Jesus did many other things as well. If every one of them were written down, I suppose that even the whole world would not have room for the books that would be written.

1: But these are written that you may believe that Jesus is the Christ, the Son of God, and that by believing you may have life in his name.

NOTE: Scripture references in order of appearance: John 20:1–19; Luke 24:37–39; John 20:20–22,24–29; Hebrews 11:1; Luke 24:44–53; John 20:30–31, NIV.

Alterations

See "Alterations" for "Words from the Cross" on page 112.

Discussion Questions

1. What stands out most in your mind after reading this script?

2. If this is a familiar story to you, did anything seem new to you this time? If so, what?

3. What does Jesus' resurrection mean to you? (Think for a moment; then answer from your heart.)

Sound Effects List

The following is a list of the sound effects contained on the accompanying compact disk in the order in which they appear on the CD along with the number of seconds for each one.

TRK	SKETCH TITLE	DESCRIPTION	DURATION
1	As Shepherds Watched Their Flocks	Background music	00:48
2	As Shepherds Watched Their Flocks	Nighttime sounds	00:25
3	As Shepherds Watched Their Flocks	Musical sounder	00:04
4	As Shepherds Watched Their Flocks	Night sounds with lamb bleating	03:30
5	As Shepherds Watched Their Flocks	Background music	01:30
6	Burnt Cookies	Knock at door	00:02
7	Burnt Cookies	Background music	01:23
8	A Father's Love	Background music	03:00
9	A Father's Love	Narrator reading with music	02:58
10	A Father's Love	Narrator and characters with music	02:50
11	I Was Thinking	Background music	01:08

12	The Jill Donapew Show	Theme music with applause	00:16
13	The Jill Donapew Show	Applause	00:09
14	The Jill Donapew Show	Voice-over: Telephone caller	00:10
15	The Jill Donapew Show	Theme music with applause	00:28
16	Mary's View of the Cross	Storm with voice-over "It is finished."	00:15
17	Nazareth Nightly News	Theme music	00:20
18	Nazareth Nightly News	Crowd noise	00:57
19	Nazareth Nightly News	Theme music	00:20
20	Pew Ponderings	Narrator's introduction	00:06
21	Pew Ponderings	Organ chords	00:07
22	Pew Ponderings	Laughter	00:07
23	Pew Ponderings	Closing hymn	00:58
24	Playing House	Background music	03:45
25	The Valentine	Musical interlude	00:08
26	The Valentine	Voice-over: Teacher	00:04
27	The Valentine	Musical interlude	00:38
28	Virtuous Woman	Background music	01:53
29	Virtuous Woman	Superhero theme music	00:11
30	The Weatherman Said	Thunderstorm	00:10
31	The Weatherman Said	Voice-over: Scripture reading	00:48
32	Words from the Cross	Background music	05:25
33	Words past the Tomb	Background music	07:40

TOTAL TIME: 42:33

Skit Subject Index

GENERAL

HOLIDAYS AND SPECIAL DAYS

Glossary

Ad libbing: Making up dialogue during a performance. While occasionally called for in the script itself, this is too often necessary when an actor forgets his or her *lines* and no *prompter* is available (a.k.a., a *director's* worst nightmare).

Act (verb): To play the role of a character in a skit or drama; to pretend to be someone other than yourself and to use actions, gestures, etc., appropriate to that person's character.

Actor's position: The physical arrangement of an actor's body in respect to the audience, usually expressed in terms of the actor's angle toward or away from the viewer *(see page 3)*.

Blocking: Determination of where individual actors will stand during various portions of a sketch and what paths they will take to change their position or location at the appropriate time *(see page 2)*.

Center stage: Area in the middle or center of the performance space used by the actors, whether that be a stage, platform, or just a specific area of the floor in front of the audience; also referred to as C in many scripts *(see page 2)*.

Cheat out: To turn the body at an outward angle facing the audience, making an actor more easily seen and heard, even if that position is not the most natural one demanded by the dialogue or action occurring at that moment *(see page 4)*.

Closed: Position of an actor's body when his or her back is either partially or completely turned toward the audience *(see page 3)*.

Costume manager: Person responsible for gathering, distributing, maintaining, and storing costumes and accessories for a drama. When an individual is skilled and the need is present, this person may also design and sew costumes *(see page 19)*.

Cross: To move across the stage from one area to another; a *stage direction* usually combined with the specific location to which the actor must cross (e.g., down left or up right); also referred to as X in many scripts *(see page 3)*.

Cue: A line spoken or action taken by another player just prior to an actor's scripted line or action *(see page 10)*.

Director: Person responsible for producing a drama, including the recruiting of actors for specific roles, coordinating rehearsals and performances, and overseeing all aspects of the *skit's* production.

Director's assistant: Person responsible for assisting the *director* in various capacities, including taking notes on the director's comments during rehearsals, prompting actors on missed cues and forgotten *lines*, and keeping actors informed of the rehearsal schedule and other important details *(see page 19)*.

Downstage: The area of the stage closest to the audience; the front of the performance area *(see page 2)*.

Focal point: A term often used in readers' theater, referring to a specific location at the rear of the performance room (e.g., sanctuary, auditorium, etc.) and above the heads of the audience, on which an actor's eyes are fixed *(see page 12)*.

In character: A phrase indicating that an actor's actions, gestures, and speech realistically portray the role he or she is playing in the given situation created by the drama. For example, if an awkward pause occurs in a performance, when another player has missed a *line*, an actor is out of character if he or she laughs, looks sideways at the *prompter*, or whispers the missed line; remaining *in character* demands that the actor continue to behave in a way consistent with the role he or she is playing—by continuing a scripted action or even *ad libbing* lines that are congruent with the personality demanded by the role.

Lines: An actor's spoken words; scripted dialogue.

Line rehearsal: Dramatic preparation in which actors rehearse only their scripted dialogue, usually as part of a larger rehearsal. This can be done quickly since physical movement and *blocking* are eliminated *(see page 5)*.

Lines-only rehearsal: A rehearsal devoted exclusively for reciting *lines,* usually without emotion or dramatic pause. This is often held just before the actual performance.

Open: Position of an actor's body when he or she faces the audience, either partially or completely *(see page 3)*.

Profile: Position of an actor's body when he or she stands at a 90-degree angle to the audience *(see page 3)*.

Projection: Volume of an actor's voice to ensure spoken *lines* are audible to all members of the audience *(see page 8)*.

Prompter: Person responsible for following the script during rehearsals and performances and for quietly reading the first words of any *line* forgotten by an actor on stage. This should be done loud enough for the actor to hear, but as quietly as possible so as not to draw the attention of the audience or distract from the performance. For this reason, the *prompter* should sit near the stage but preferably out of the audience's view.

Props: See *properties.*

Properties: Objects used by actors in a drama, usually smaller than *set pieces.* These may include costume accessories when such accessories are used for *stage business* (e.g., setting a watch or fumbling through a purse).

Properties manager: Person responsible for all *properties* needed in a particular *sketch,* including gathering, storage, distribution, and appropriate placement of such objects on stage *(see page 19)*.

Read-through: Dramatic preparation in which actors read the entire script aloud. This can be done before or after parts have been assigned, but should occur at least once before beginning the *blocking* of the *sketch (see page 24)*.

Readers' theater: Formal style of dramatic presentation that emphasizes words over action, using the actors' voices much like a choir; involves no *props* or costumes, and players read from the script rather than memorize their lines *(see page 12)*.

Role play: To assume the persona of a character and *act* as that character would, in *ad-libbed* movement and dialogue, with little direction as to the setting and circumstances being played out; often a useful dramatic exercise *(see page 22).*

Run-through: Dramatic preparation in which all elements of a *sketch* are rehearsed from beginning to end, including all *lines, blocking,* and *stage business (see page 24).*

Scene: Smaller portion of a *sketch,* usually marked by a fixed setting and a sense of continuous time. For example, one *scene* in a *skit* may involve two characters talking in school on a Monday morning; the subsequent *scene* might show one of those characters at home talking to her mother later that day. *Scene* may also refer to the setting of a drama and the performance area with all of its *set pieces.*

Set pieces: Furniture and other large items used in a sketch that begin in a fixed location on stage.

Sketch: A short comedy or drama, usually with a particular theme; also *skit.*

Skit: A short comedy or drama, usually with a particular theme; also *sketch.*

Stage area(s): Geographical location(s) on the performance area, such as down left, up center, or right center, and typically abbreviated in the *stage directions (see page 2).*

Stage business: Small movements of an actor that may or may not require a change in location. Used to make the players look natural and more believable, these actions should be *in character* for each actor's role. For example, a character in a hurry may check her watch quickly, put it to her ear to be sure it is working, and even tap on the face of the watch; a character who is nervous might shift his weight from one foot to the other and repeatedly push his glasses up on his nose *(see page 1).*

Stage directions: Instructions indicating an actor's location on stage. These are given simply by specifying the actor's character and a particular *stage area,* such as down left (DL) *(see page 2).*

Stage manager: Person responsible for all *set pieces,* including moving them on and off stage for rehearsals and performances, with the actors' help as needed; may also assist the *properties manager* in placing *props* on the stage *(see page 19).*

Take board: Rectangular piece of wood, often with a chalkboard material on the front surface, that has a long, thin piece of wood across the top and is hinged on one side, commonly used in television and movie production to separate *run-throughs* for film editing purposes. The title of a performance (a *sketch,* for the purpose of this book) is written on the front of the board; the top board is snapped shut with the announcement of that title, followed by the words, "Take one (or whatever number is appropriate)" *(see page 15).*

Upstage (adj./adv.): The area of the stage farthest from the audience; the back of the performance area *(see page 2).*

Upstage (verb): To stand farther to the back of the performance area, forcing a *downstage* actor to turn away from the audience in a more *closed* position in order to interact with the *upstage* actor *(see page 4).*

Voice-over: For the purposes of this book, an audio term referring to prerecorded *lines* that are played over a sound system, sometimes with music or other sound effects heard in the background. For a list of the *voice-overs* included on the companion compact disk, see the "Sound Effects List" on page 117.

Walk-through: Dramatic preparation in which actors read from their scripts as they move through their *blocking* on stage. During this type of rehearsal, a *director* may modify the original blocking and have the actors experiment with different positions and locations *(see page 24).*

Wing(s): Area(s) offstage from which actors commonly make their entrances and exits, typically to the right and left of the performance area. Because it is here that actors await their *cues* while other characters are performing, the *wings* should hide the waiting players from the view of the audience *(see page 15).*